McCALL-C

Standard Test Lessons in Reading

Book E

WILLIAM A. McCALL, Ph.D.
Professor Emeritus of Education
Teachers College, Columbia University

LELAH CRABBS SCHROEDER, Ph.D.
Formerly Assistant Professor of Education
Teachers College, Columbia University

Revised under the editorial supervision of
ROBERT P. STARR. Ed.D.

TEACHERS COLLEGE PRESS

Teachers College, Columbia University
New York and London

Swat one male and one female fly in early spring, and you will kill about 340,000,000,000,000 flies that they and their young would have produced by the end of the summer. Let live a spider that you are about to kill, and it will keep from being born more flies than the stars you can see on a clear night. Keep alive one bird or a lizard, and you will have prevented the birth of a billion times a billion flies. If there were no natural enemies of flies, the world would be covered with them.

Why kill flies? On their sticky feet and hairy bodies, and in their mouths, they carry many millions of germs and bring some forty kinds of disease. They are born in filth and bring that filth to you.

So swat the fly! But better still, protect its enemies and clean up its breeding places.

1

1. **Perfectly clean living conditions would prevent the spread of**
   Ⓐ flowers   Ⓑ health   Ⓒ disease   Ⓓ lizards
2. **The fly is our**   Ⓐ enemy   Ⓑ friend   Ⓒ destroyer   Ⓓ helper
3. **The fly's body is**   Ⓐ beautiful   Ⓑ hard   Ⓒ smooth   Ⓓ hairy
4. **The feet of the fly are**   Ⓐ long   Ⓑ pointed   Ⓒ sticky   Ⓓ satiny
5. **Flies breed in places that are**   Ⓐ clean   Ⓑ beautiful   Ⓒ filthy   Ⓓ cold
6. **What should you do to flies?**   Ⓐ kill them   Ⓑ wash them   Ⓒ feed them   Ⓓ guard them
7. **What should you do to most spiders? Let them**   Ⓐ die   Ⓑ hang   Ⓒ live   Ⓓ bite
8. **What are lizards to flies?**   Ⓐ friends   Ⓑ enemies   Ⓒ alike   Ⓓ diseased

No. right	1	2	3	4	5	6	7	8
G score	2.6	3.0	3.5	4.0	4.6	5.2	5.8	6.6

2

Did you ever hear a real cuckoo bird? It makes a sound that is very much like the striking of a cuckoo clock, but much sweeter. When you hear the first notes of the cuckoo bird, you will know that winter has gone and spring has come again.

The cuckoo bird never builds a nest of its own but lays its tiny egg in another bird's nest. The other bird hatches that egg with its own, and the little birds grow up together. The mother bird does not seem to notice that one of the birds is not like the others. She brings food for all of them, but the young cuckoo bird, which is the largest of all, usually eats most of the food.

1. **This story tells how a cuckoo** Ⓐ builds its nest Ⓑ feeds itself
    Ⓒ flies Ⓓ lays its egg
2. **The song of the real cuckoo is** Ⓐ louder than a cuckoo clock
    Ⓑ sweeter than a cuckoo clock Ⓒ softer than a cuckoo clock
    Ⓓ harsher than a cuckoo clock
3. **The song of the cuckoo foretells** Ⓐ summer Ⓑ winter Ⓒ autumn
    Ⓓ spring
4. **The cuckoo bird builds a nest** Ⓐ usually Ⓑ always Ⓒ never
    Ⓓ sometimes
5. **How many eggs does the cuckoo bird lay in each nest?** Ⓐ one
    Ⓑ two Ⓒ three Ⓓ four
6. **In the nest the young cuckoo is the** Ⓐ largest Ⓑ smallest
    Ⓒ tallest Ⓓ youngest
7. **The mother bird brings food to** Ⓐ one bird Ⓑ the cuckoo bird
    Ⓒ her birds Ⓓ all the birds
8. **Who eats most of the food?** Ⓐ the little birds Ⓑ the mother bird
    Ⓒ the young cuckoo Ⓓ the father bird

No. right	1	2	3	4	5	6	7	8
G score	3.3	3.7	4.1	4.6	5.1	5.6	6.1	6.7

Their airplane had been forced down at sea. They barely had time to inflate the yellow rubber dinghies and climb into them before the plane sank. Would a rescue plane find them? One did at last. To the great surprise of the anxious watchers, they saw a boat hanging under it. The boat was aimed and dropped from the plane. Parachutes opened and let it down gently about a hundred yards from the dinghies. A sea anchor shot from the front. A long, light line shot from each side.

When the men pulled themselves into the boat by these lines, they found it equipped with two outboard motors, sails, compass, charts, waterproofed instructions for everything in four languages, dry clothes, food, cigarettes, knives, fishing tackle—everything but a welcome mat. All this was provided to make sure that they would keep afloat and alive until they could make harbor or be rescued.

3

1. **What happened to the unlucky airplane? It**   Ⓐ exploded   Ⓑ fell apart in the air   Ⓒ ran out of gas   Ⓓ was forced down
2. **Where did this airplane in trouble land?**   Ⓐ in a tree   Ⓑ in a field   Ⓒ in the water   Ⓓ on the desert
3. **The rescuing airplane dropped**   Ⓐ a shell   Ⓑ a boat   Ⓒ a dinghy   Ⓓ messages
4. **Directions for using equipment were supplied in how many languages?**   Ⓐ two   Ⓑ four   Ⓒ five   Ⓓ six
5. **The rescue boat was let down from the airplane by**   Ⓐ parachutes   Ⓑ light rope   Ⓒ cable   Ⓓ balloon
6. **How many motors did the rescue boat have?**   Ⓐ one   Ⓑ two   Ⓒ three   Ⓓ four
7. **How were the printed instructions protected from destruction by water? They were**   Ⓐ wrapped in cloth   Ⓑ printed on metal   Ⓒ water-proofed   Ⓓ put in a glass jar
8. **The boat's equipment would help these men to**   Ⓐ reach safety   Ⓑ find their airplane   Ⓒ learn to speak a new language   Ⓓ repair their airplane

No. right	1	2	3	4	5	6	7	8
G score	3.1	3.6	4.1	4.6	5.3	6.0	6.7	7.4

4

I live in Chicago and I am a window-washer. People used to say to me, "Look, Susan, you're thirty-five years old. Why don't you put both feet on the ground and settle down?" But I'm not interested. Life is too exciting, hanging in the air outside the windows on the fiftieth floor. The noisy, rushing, pushy city is so far below, it seems like a quiet children's game. There's nothing but the sky and the shlurp of the window brushes to keep me company. I guess I'm part bird, and this high-altitude work is the next best thing to flying.

1. **The author lives** Ⓐ in the country Ⓑ on the fiftieth floor Ⓒ in New York City Ⓓ in Chicago
2. **To make a living, the author** Ⓐ writes stories Ⓑ feeds birds Ⓒ paints Ⓓ washes windows
3. **How do Susan's friends feel about her profession?** Ⓐ excited Ⓑ uninterested Ⓒ supportive Ⓓ disapproving
4. **The author is** Ⓐ happy at her job Ⓑ pushy Ⓒ afraid of heights Ⓓ not interested in her friends
5. **From where she works, the city** Ⓐ looks exciting Ⓑ is settled down Ⓒ seems like a quiet children's game Ⓓ scares her
6. **The things that keep Susan company at work are** Ⓐ birds Ⓑ her friends Ⓒ other window-washers Ⓓ the sky and the sound of her brushes
7. **Susan says she is part bird because** Ⓐ she has wings Ⓑ she can fly Ⓒ she likes to sing Ⓓ she likes working high in the air
8. **Choose the best title:** Ⓐ My Life in the Tree Tops Ⓑ Susan, the Street Sweeper Ⓒ Susan Learns to Fly Ⓓ The Joys of Window-Washing

No. right	1	2	3	4	5	6	7	8
G score	2.3	2.6	3.3	4.0	4.7	5.7	6.6	7.6

A 250-foot Douglas fir towering toward the sky must be cut very carefully. A high-climbing lumberjack straps spurs on his feet, ties a single loop of rope around the huge trunk of the tree and his waist, and, pushing up the loop as he climbs, starts up the tree on his dangerous job. Each limb, as he saws it off, falls with a great crash. When he is up nearly two hundred feet, he is ready to cut and saw off about fifty feet of the fir's top. If the top falls toward him, he may be crushed. If the trunk splits, it may pull the loop tight and squeeze him to death. He knows all this and therefore works carefully. At last the saw is nearly through. The top trembles and falls, giving the trunk such a kick that it sways back and forth for fifty feet, making the man dizzy. When it stops swaying, he climbs to the cut end of the trunk and lies down on it to rest before beginning the long journey back to the ground.

5

1. **The tree is**   Ⓐ tall   Ⓑ short   Ⓒ squat   Ⓓ young
2. **Which tree is this article about?**   Ⓐ maple   Ⓑ oak   Ⓒ elm   Ⓓ Douglas fir
3. **A high-climber must be**   Ⓐ curious   Ⓑ brave   Ⓒ tall   Ⓓ careless
4. **About how many feet from the ground is the climber when he saws off the tree's top?**   Ⓐ fifty   Ⓑ one hundred   Ⓒ two hundred   Ⓓ three hundred
5. **About how many feet of the tree's top are cut off?**   Ⓐ twenty   Ⓑ thirty   Ⓒ forty   Ⓓ fifty
6. **What part of the tree sways back and forth?**   Ⓐ the top   Ⓑ the branches   Ⓒ the trunk   Ⓓ the leaves
7. **The swaying makes the climber**   Ⓐ dizzy   Ⓑ sick   Ⓒ happy   Ⓓ angry
8. **What does this tree climber strap on his feet?**   Ⓐ boots   Ⓑ leggings   Ⓒ ropes   Ⓓ spurs

No. right	1	2	3	4	5	6	7	8
G score	2.6	3.2	3.8	4.5	5.3	6.2	7.2	8.1

6

Have you ever heard the music called *Scenes From Childhood*? If you play the piano, you may learn it one day.

The composer was named Robert Schumann. He lived in Germany in the early 1800s. He loved the piano very much. He composed most of his music for the piano.

A very talented woman lived at the same time. Her name was Clara Wieck. She played the piano so well that she gave concerts and became famous. Robert and Clara fell in love and married.

Both were great musicians, and both are remembered now, but Clara Schumann was much more famous then. Sometimes people called Robert "Mr. Clara Schumann." They were teasing, but he wasn't happy about this name.

1. **Clara played the**   Ⓐ piano   Ⓑ drums   Ⓒ flute   Ⓓ violin
2. **Clara and Robert lived in**   Ⓐ the early 1900s   Ⓑ the late 1900s   Ⓒ the early 1800s   Ⓓ the late 1800s
3. **Robert Schumann was a**   Ⓐ singer   Ⓑ composer   Ⓒ drummer   Ⓓ doctor
4. **Clara was famous because she**   Ⓐ was a composer   Ⓑ was in love   Ⓒ was a child   Ⓓ gave concerts
5. **This selection is about**   Ⓐ a famous composer   Ⓑ a famous pianist   Ⓒ two great musicians   Ⓓ *Scenes From Childhood*
6. **The Schumanns lived in**   Ⓐ Germany   Ⓑ the United States   Ⓒ France   Ⓓ England
7. *Scenes From Childhood* **is**   Ⓐ flute music   Ⓑ a play   Ⓒ a book about Robert   Ⓓ piano music
8. **Which statement is true?**   Ⓐ When they lived, Robert was more famous than Clara.   Ⓑ When they lived, Clara was more famous than Robert.   Ⓒ Neither musician was famous.   Ⓓ Only Robert was talented.

No. right	1	2	3	4	5	6	7	8
G score	2.3	2.6	3.3	4.0	4.8	5.8	6.8	7.8

The year was 1816. Baron Karl Drais von Sauerbronn invented a velocipede. At first, it seemed like a great idea. It would help people get around better. His velocipede had handlebars and wheels, but it had no pedals. To make it stop and go, people had to use their feet. No wonder no one got very excited about this first kind of bicycle! The Baron named his invention the *draisine,* but most people just called it a dandy horse.

In 1839, Kirkpatrick MacMillan, a Scottish blacksmith, invented the foot pedal for the bicycle. He wanted to show off his invention, so he took a ride into town. On the way, he knocked over a child. He received a fine for causing an accident. MacMillan is not just famous for inventing the first real bicycle. He also had the first bicycle accident!

1. **The baron built his invention in** Ⓐ 1812 Ⓑ 1742 Ⓒ 1816 Ⓓ 1920
2. **The first bicycle had no** Ⓐ pedals Ⓑ handlebars Ⓒ wheels Ⓓ rider
3. **A velocipede is a** Ⓐ car Ⓑ bicycle Ⓒ plane Ⓓ wind
4. **After MacMillan knocked over a child, he** Ⓐ invented the foot pedal Ⓑ invented the bicycle Ⓒ received a fine Ⓓ took a ride
5. **The *draisine* was** Ⓐ invented by the Baron Karl Drais von Sauerbronn Ⓑ a kind of eye drop Ⓒ a kind of horse Ⓓ a foot pedal
6. **Kirkpatrick MacMillan was** Ⓐ a Scottish lord Ⓑ a Scottish blacksmith Ⓒ a Baron Ⓓ inventor of the *draisine*
7. **No one got excited about the *draisine* because** Ⓐ it had such a funny name Ⓑ it didn't do anything Ⓒ it cost too much money Ⓓ riders had to stop and start it with their feet
8. **Choose the best title:** Ⓐ The *Draisine* Ⓑ The First Bicycles Ⓒ Wheels Within Wheels Ⓓ After Kirkpatrick MacMillan

No. right	1	2	3	4	5	6	7	8
G score	3.3	3.8	4.4	5.1	5.8	6.7	7.4	8.3

8

Tommy lives in Browning, Montana. Browning is the only town in the Blackfeet Indian Reservation. It isn't a big town. There are a few shops where tourists can buy things the Blackfeet have made. There is a pencil factory, and there is a good museum.

Tommy's mother works at the museum. His father works in the pencil factory. When Tommy isn't at school, he makes things for the tourists.

The Blackfeet got their name because many of them wore dark moccasins. They quickly learned to ride the horses brought to this country by the Spanish explorers. For many years they roamed over the great northwest plains hunting the buffalo. Today they live in a little corner of that land at the foot of the Rocky Mountains.

1. **Browning, Montana,** Ⓐ is a big town   Ⓑ is the name of an Indian reservation   Ⓒ has no factories   Ⓓ is at the foot of the Rocky Mountains
2. **Tommy**   Ⓐ hunts buffalo   Ⓑ works at the museum   Ⓒ lives in Browning   Ⓓ does not go to school
3. **The Spanish explorers**   Ⓐ killed the buffalo   Ⓑ live with the Blackfeet   Ⓒ brought horses to this country   Ⓓ roamed over the plains hunting buffalo
4. **Tommy's mother**   Ⓐ works at the museum   Ⓑ makes things for the tourists   Ⓒ works at the pencil factory   Ⓓ teaches school
5. **The Blackfeet got their name**   Ⓐ because of their black feet   Ⓑ from the Apache Indians   Ⓒ from the Spanish explorers   Ⓓ because of the moccasins they wore
6. **Today the Blackfeet**   Ⓐ hunt buffalo   Ⓑ all work in shops   Ⓒ roam the plains   Ⓓ live on an Indian reservation
7. **For many years the Blackfeet**   Ⓐ roamed over the southwest plains   Ⓑ roamed over the northwest plains   Ⓒ lived in the Rocky Mountains   Ⓓ roamed over the northeast plains
8. **In Browning, Montana, there is**   Ⓐ a pencil factory   Ⓑ a blacksmith shop   Ⓒ no museum   Ⓓ no school

No. right	1	2	3	4	5	6	7	8
G score	3.3	3.8	4.5	5.2	5.9	6.8	7.6	8.4

Tommy's mother knows the history of the Blackfeet Indians. Her work at the reservation museum helps to keep their past alive.

The Blackfeet were well known for riding, hunting, and fighting. They fought other Indians and white men to keep their land. They fought very hard, but the United States was growing. Soon there were too many white men to fight.

The buffalo began to vanish, too. The Blackfeet depended on the buffalo for food, clothing, and shelter. They even used the bones for tools and decorations. Then, men like "Buffalo" Bill killed the animals for sport, often hundreds of them in a day. Soon there were not enough buffalo to keep the Blackfeet alive. They were forced to trade beaver skins and the beautiful things they made in order to survive. Their way of life had changed forever.

1. **The Blackfeet were well known for**   Ⓐ killing buffalo for sport   Ⓑ trading beaver skins   Ⓒ riding, hunting, and fighting   Ⓓ food, clothing, and shelter
2. **Who did the Blackfeet fight?**   Ⓐ only other Indians   Ⓑ Indians and whites   Ⓒ only white men   Ⓓ nobody
3. **Tommy's mother**   Ⓐ kills animals for sport   Ⓑ helps to keep the United States growing   Ⓒ makes tools from buffalo bones   Ⓓ helps preserve the tribe's history
4. **The Blackfeet depended on buffalo for**   Ⓐ food only   Ⓑ fighting   Ⓒ trading their skins   Ⓓ food, clothing, and shelter
5. **Why did the Blackfeet fight?**   Ⓐ to kill the buffalo   Ⓑ to trade beaver skins   Ⓒ to save their land   Ⓓ for sport
6. **Buffalo Bill killed**   Ⓐ the Blackfeet   Ⓑ all the buffalo   Ⓒ thousands of buffalo in a day   Ⓓ the buffalo for sport
7. **The Blackfeet were forced to**   Ⓐ trade buffalo skins   Ⓑ vanish   Ⓒ work in museums   Ⓓ change their way of life
8. **Choose the best title:**   Ⓐ Tommy's Mother   Ⓑ Working at the Museum   Ⓒ Buffalo Bill   Ⓓ Changing Times for the Blackfeet

No. right	1	2	3	4	5	6	7	8
G score	3.4	3.8	4.4	5.0	5.6	6.2	7.0	7.6

10

Today, many of the Blackfeet Indians work at the pencil factory in Browning. Tommy's father works there putting together slats of wood. The slats sandwich eight pieces of graphite. These slats are later cut into eight pencils. Tommy's father is proud of the job he does. It isn't easy work. What he likes best about the job is that it lasts all year round.

Before there was a pencil factory, Tommy's father worked as a lumberjack in the mountains. The winters in Montana are long and hard, so all winter long he could not work. Now that he works at the factory, his family has enough money. They were able to move to a nice house. Tommy's mother has a good kitchen, and Tommy has his own room now.

Life is very different for Tommy than it was for his great, great, great grandfather who lived by hunting and trading, and whose home was made of buffalo skins.

1. **Tommy's father now works**   Ⓐ in the mountains   Ⓑ at the pencil factory   Ⓒ as a lumberjack   Ⓓ only part of the year
2. **The slats of wood sandwich**   Ⓐ the pencils together   Ⓑ ten pieces of graphite   Ⓒ eight pencils   Ⓓ eight pieces of graphite
3. **The winters in Montana are**   Ⓐ long and hard   Ⓑ short and mild   Ⓒ short and hard   Ⓓ long and mild
4. **What does Tommy's father like best about his job?**   Ⓐ the work is easy   Ⓑ it is a year-round job   Ⓒ he doesn't work in the winter   Ⓓ he can walk to work
5. **Tommy's mother has**   Ⓐ no job   Ⓑ several children   Ⓒ a good kitchen   Ⓓ her own room
6. **Tommy's father used to**   Ⓐ work as a lumberjack   Ⓑ live in the mountains   Ⓒ hunt buffalo   Ⓓ trade
7. **Tommy has**   Ⓐ his own room   Ⓑ a good job   Ⓒ a large allowance   Ⓓ a buffalo skin
8. **Tommy's great, great, great grandfather**   Ⓐ lived in the mountains   Ⓑ worked in a factory   Ⓒ was a lumberjack   Ⓓ made his home from buffalo skins

No. right	1	2	3	4	5	6	7	8
G score	3.1	3.6	4.1	4.6	5.3	6.0	6.8	7.4

The rat is more dangerous to man than the rattlesnake, lion, or tiger. The rat lives in old barns and buildings, under houses or porches, and sometimes in basements. It carries and spreads such diseases as typhus, tularemia, rabies, ratbite fever, pneumonia, and bubonic plague.

Rats are undesirable for other reasons. They are very destructive. They have been known to gnaw lead pipes, wood, soap, fabrics, book covers, and valuable papers. They also eat just about every food man does. They kill young chickens and even cats.

There are over a hundred million of these pests in the United States, and they are multiplying faster than they are being killed. Were it not for their enemies, the descendants of one pair of rats would number 350,000,000 in three years. When a county in Texas set out to exterminate rats, 153,720 tails were turned in during a six-week period.

Perhaps your class will lead a drive against rats by trapping or poisoning them with something that will not harm other animals.

1. **The animal most dangerous to man is the**   Ⓐ tiger   Ⓑ lion   Ⓒ rat   Ⓓ rattlesnake
2. **The most important reason for killing rats is protection against**   Ⓐ dangerous diseases   Ⓑ loss of valuable papers   Ⓒ loss of chickens   Ⓓ loss of pets
3. **About how many of these pests are there in the United States? Over**   Ⓐ 1,000   Ⓑ 100,000   Ⓒ 100,000,000   Ⓓ 1,000,000,000
4. **If your city has 50,000 rats living in it now, and nothing is done to kill them, next year there will be**   Ⓐ fewer   Ⓑ the same number   Ⓒ a few more   Ⓓ thousands more
5. **When an extermination campaign was conducted in Texas, how many rat tails were turned in?**   Ⓐ 720   Ⓑ 53,000   Ⓒ 153,720   Ⓓ 15,372,000
6. **How long did Texas conduct its war against rats?**   Ⓐ one week   Ⓑ one year   Ⓒ six weeks   Ⓓ the text does not state
7. **Rat tails were turned in because**   Ⓐ they proved all rats had tails   Ⓑ they showed how many rats had been killed   Ⓒ the county wanted rat tails   Ⓓ rats without tails are harmless
8. **When exterminating rats, we must guard against also destroying**   Ⓐ other animals   Ⓑ shrubs   Ⓒ furniture   Ⓓ barns

No. right	1	2	3	4	5	6	7	8
G score	3.6	4.1	4.7	5.4	6.1	6.9	7.6	8.4

12

Unexplained lights have puzzled people for many years. The Texas ghost light is a mysterious light that shines from a peak in southwest Texas. Nearby settlers saw this light more than a hundred years ago, and travelers along Highway 90 between Alpine and Marfa, Texas, still report seeing it. The light does not always shine from the same place but moves from point to point on the peak. So far, no one has solved the mystery of the Texas ghost light.

Often strange brown lights have been seen in the deep valley below Blowing Rock, North Carolina. These also move about. Scientists have tried to solve this mystery too, but without success.

One day a woman who lives in a house high above this valley was resting in bed. The sun was shining. There was not a cloud in the sky. The window was raised several inches. Suddenly a ball of light squeezed through this window opening, knocked the woman unconscious, and burned her in a way no doctor had ever seen before.

1. **Choose the best title:**   Ⓐ Traveling Through Texas   Ⓑ Our Sun Is the Strongest of All Lights   Ⓒ Examples of Unexplained Strange Lights   Ⓓ How a Lady in North Carolina Was Burned
2. **On the day the woman was burned**   Ⓐ the sun was shining   Ⓑ the sky was cloudy   Ⓒ there was little light   Ⓓ it was very warm
3. **The Texas light**   Ⓐ grows brighter   Ⓑ changes color   Ⓒ stays the same   Ⓓ moves about
4. **The most certain thing about the Texas ghost light is that it is**   Ⓐ a uranium deposit   Ⓑ fox fire   Ⓒ a mystery   Ⓓ caused by swamp gas
5. **At the time the woman in North Carolina was burned, she was**   Ⓐ cleaning house   Ⓑ resting in bed   Ⓒ riding in her car   Ⓓ taking a bath
6. **The ball of light squeezed through the**   Ⓐ ceiling   Ⓑ raised window   Ⓒ floor cracks   Ⓓ cloud
7. **Which was burned? The**   Ⓐ settlers   Ⓑ scientists   Ⓒ house   Ⓓ woman
8. **The North Carolina light is**   Ⓐ a hoax   Ⓑ a mystery   Ⓒ a new event   Ⓓ no longer seen

No. right	1	2	3	4	5	6	7	8
G score	3.0	3.6	4.2	4.8	5.6	6.5	7.3	8.1

Who is the greatest athlete in the world? Since 1912 the title is usually thought to belong to the most recent Olympic decathlon champion. That year King Gustav V of Sweden told Jim Thorpe, the decathlon gold medal winner, "Sir, you are the greatest athlete in the world." Thorpe replied, "Thanks, King."

Bruce Jenner won the decathlon at the Montreal Olympics in 1976. Even though Queen Elizabeth II of England didn't speak to him, many agree that he deserves to be known as the world's greatest athlete. His winning score in the ten events was 8,618, the highest ever made by anyone anywhere. The previous world record that he broke (8,524) was his own.

When Jenner attended Sleepy Hollow High School in Tarrytown, New York, and later in Newton, Connecticut, he played football, basketball, baseball, and water skied. What most people do not know about the champion is that in those days he didn't excel in any sport. It took years of training and practice for him to get to the top.

13

1. **Who made the royal decree that named the greatest athlete in the world?** Ⓐ Queen Elizabeth Ⓑ Jim Thorpe Ⓒ King Gustav Ⓓ Bruce Jenner
2. **The greatest athlete in the world is whoever** Ⓐ wins an Olympic championship Ⓑ wins the decathlon gold medal at the Olympics Ⓒ plays the best game in Montreal Ⓓ is the King of Sweden
3. **Jim Thorpe won the decathlon in** Ⓐ 1976 Ⓑ 1918 Ⓒ 1912 Ⓓ high school
4. **How many events make up the decathlon?** Ⓐ 12 Ⓑ 8,824 Ⓒ 10 Ⓓ 8,618
5. **Where did Bruce Jenner win his gold medal?** Ⓐ in Montreal Ⓑ in Sweden Ⓒ in England Ⓓ in Olympia
6. **His winning score in 1976** Ⓐ broke his old record by 100 points Ⓑ was 8,524 Ⓒ tied the previous world record Ⓓ was the highest ever made by anyone
7. **In high school, Bruce Jenner** Ⓐ ran races Ⓑ was sleepy Ⓒ got to the top Ⓓ wasn't an outstanding athelete
8. **To become a gold medal winner, Bruce Jenner had to** Ⓐ play baseball, football, and basketball Ⓑ train long and hard Ⓒ be told he was the greatest athlete in the world Ⓓ be a champion in high school

No. right	1	2	3	4	5	6	7	8
G score	3.8	4.4	5.0	5.6	6.3	7.0	7.7	8.6

14

One day, while watching the fish in an aquarium, I became interested in their tireless activities. Then I wondered just how much I knew about fish, their habits, and their development. I decided that my education needed expanding. I sought an encyclopedia and learned many things.

For example, I found that fish propel themselves by their tails and guide their course by means of their fins. They are of various colors. The main color usually affords self-protection. They are of various shapes and sizes and have many peculiar characteristics.

Some fish make a noise, some are poisonous, some have teeth, some can climb a tree for five or seven feet, and some can fly through the air for perhaps a quarter of a mile after lifting themselves from the water. Don't some of these things seem almost impossible?

There are about thirteen thousand species of fish, large and small, some weighing as much as a thousand pounds. Some are very long like the shark, which sometimes measures fifty feet.

1. **This selection is chiefly about**   Ⓐ the author   Ⓑ an aquarium   Ⓒ fish   Ⓓ an encyclopedia
2. **Which statement is correct?**   Ⓐ All fish have the same characteristics.   Ⓑ I found nothing unusual about the characteristics of fish.   Ⓒ Characteristics of fish are very ordinary.   Ⓓ Fish have many peculiar characteristics.
3. **The author's information was gained by**   Ⓐ watching the activities of the fish   Ⓑ inquiring from his friends   Ⓒ wondering about it   Ⓓ consulting a reference book
4. **Fish use their tails to**   Ⓐ guide their course   Ⓑ keep themselves afloat   Ⓒ propel themselves through the water   Ⓓ protect themselves from the enemy
5. **The main color of fish usually serves**   Ⓐ to make them beautiful   Ⓑ for self-protection   Ⓒ to attract attention   Ⓓ no purpose whatever
6. **There is a certain species of fish that can fly all of**   Ⓐ a hundred feet   Ⓑ a quarter of a mile   Ⓒ five hundred feet   Ⓓ many miles
7. **The selection informs us that**   Ⓐ some fish have teeth   Ⓑ usually fish have teeth   Ⓒ the majority of fish possess teeth   Ⓓ it is essential that fish have teeth
8. **As a result of his interest in fish, the author learned**   Ⓐ practically nothing   Ⓑ entirely too much   Ⓒ a sufficient amount   Ⓓ many things

No. right	1	2	3	4	5	6	7	8
G score	4.4	4.9	5.4	5.9	6.5	7.1	7.6	8.2

When school was not in session, we three brothers worked in the mines with our father. He was particularly expert in diagnosing the condition of the rock under which we worked and in detecting the imminence of danger. For this reason he was always assigned to the dangerous task of removing the last coal that supported the over-hanging rock. As more and more of the coal was removed, the weight of the millions of tons of rock slowly settled upon the frail wooden timbers. They became taut like the strings of a violin, so that flying splinters caused by the pressure made a sort of music. Occasionally, a timber would break with a sharp sound like the crack of a rifle. Through it all, father worked as though unhearing. Perhaps a week later he would say, "Get your tools, boys, and get out as fast as you can." We would go a short distance to a place of safety, lie down behind a car so as not to be struck by loose objects blown by the wind of the fall, and listen to the snapping of the props and the grinding of the mountain. As we grew older, we, too, learned to interpret hints given by the rock.

15

1. **The father was expert in**   Ⓐ interpreting the strength of the rock   Ⓑ playing the violin   Ⓒ grinding up the coal   Ⓓ ignoring danger
2. **What made a sharp sound?**   Ⓐ a rifle   Ⓑ the tools   Ⓒ splinters   Ⓓ breaking props
3. **According to the selection, the father worked**   Ⓐ in a safe job   Ⓑ as though unhearing   Ⓒ only at night   Ⓓ heedlessly
4. **"The imminence of danger" means that danger was**   Ⓐ remote   Ⓑ near at hand   Ⓒ a mile away   Ⓓ past
5. **The selection shows that the work of mining coal is**   Ⓐ dangerous   Ⓑ pleasant   Ⓒ healthful   Ⓓ remunerative
6. **The props were made of**   Ⓐ steel   Ⓑ wood   Ⓒ concrete   Ⓓ brick
7. **The selection states that the props were like violin strings because they were**   Ⓐ long   Ⓑ frail   Ⓒ struck a blow   Ⓓ taut
8. **Why would the father tell his sons to run?**   Ⓐ he could tell there was going to be a cave-in   Ⓑ he was blown down by the wind   Ⓒ he wanted them to get in the car   Ⓓ he didn't want them to get splinters

No. right	1	2	3	4	5	6	7	8
G score	4.0	4.6	5.2	5.8	6.5	7.2	7.9	8.8

16

Have you ever wondered why plants are green? It may seem to be an unimportant question, but if plants weren't green, there wouldn't be any life on this planet. The green color is caused by a chemical called chlorophyll. Chlorophyll is the only chemical able to turn the energy of sunlight into food for the plant. The plant also uses water and carbon dioxide to produce food and oxygen. Plants breathe out oxygen and breathe in carbon dioxide. People breathe out carbon dioxide and breathe in oxygen. This very basic balance is made possible by chlorophyll.

1. **If plants weren't green, they wouldn't be able to**   Ⓐ breathe in oxygen   Ⓑ use water   Ⓒ live   Ⓓ make carbon dioxide
2. **Plants are green because of**   Ⓐ chlorophyll   Ⓑ sunlight   Ⓒ oxygen   Ⓓ carbon dioxide
3. **What turns sunlight into food for plants?**   Ⓐ oxygen   Ⓑ water   Ⓒ chlorophyll   Ⓓ carbon dioxide
4. **Plants breathe in**   Ⓐ oxygen   Ⓑ chlorophyll   Ⓒ water   Ⓓ carbon dioxide
5. **Plants breathe out**   Ⓐ oxygen   Ⓑ chlorophyll   Ⓒ water   Ⓓ carbon dioxide
6. **What are two things plants use to make food?**   Ⓐ water and oxygen   Ⓑ chlorophyll and carbon   Ⓒ water and carbon dioxide   Ⓓ chlorophyll and oxygen
7. **If it weren't for chlorophyll, there would be no**   Ⓐ sunlight   Ⓑ life on Earth   Ⓒ water   Ⓓ Earth
8. **Choose the best title:**   Ⓐ This Green Planet   Ⓑ Oxygen and You   Ⓒ Chlorophyll: A Key to Life   Ⓓ Growing Plants

No. right	1	2	3	4	5	6	7	8
G score	3.7	4.2	4.7	5.4	6.1	6.9	7.6	8.4

Probably the most famous mummy in the world is King Tut's. King Tutankhamun, which was his real name, was an Egyptian king who lived about 3300 years ago. When archeologists discovered his tomb in 1922, they found many ancient treasures including his body which had been kept whole by a secret process.

Specially trained people who prepared the bodies for burial were called embalmers. The first thing the embalmers did was remove the brain. As strange as it seems, they did this through the nose. Then they took out the other organs of the body. These were put in jars to be placed in the tomb with the body.

Next the embalmers used a chemical to dry the body out. When it was very dry, they wrapped it in layers and layers of linen bandages. Finally the body was ready to be buried. They put it into a coffin that often had a face painted on it to look like the person inside. This was called a death mask. The beautiful death mask of King Tut was found along with his mummy when archeologists discovered his tomb.

1. **King Tut's real name was** Ⓐ Tutly   Ⓑ Tutankhamun   Ⓒ Thutmose   Ⓓ Tutman

2. **King Tut lived** Ⓐ 3300 years ago   Ⓑ 1000 years ago   Ⓒ 100 years ago   Ⓓ 10,000 years ago

3. **King Tut was** Ⓐ an embalmer   Ⓑ a ruler of Egypt   Ⓒ an archeologist   Ⓓ a secret process

4. **An archeologist is someone who** Ⓐ prepares bodies for burial Ⓑ builds tombs   Ⓒ looks for things left by people who lived long ago Ⓓ paints coffins

5. **The secret process to prepare bodies for burial is called** Ⓐ notifying Ⓑ mummifying   Ⓒ bandaging   Ⓓ analyzing

6. **The first thing the embalmers did when they were preparing a body was to** Ⓐ place it in a coffin   Ⓑ paint a death mask   Ⓒ wrap it in linen bandages   Ⓓ remove the brain through the nose

7. **The organs taken out of the body were** Ⓐ thrown into the sea Ⓑ placed in jars   Ⓒ put in the coffin   Ⓓ buried in a deep hole

8. **In order to dry the body out, the embalmers used** Ⓐ the sun   Ⓑ a hot oven   Ⓒ warm air   Ⓓ a chemical

No. right	1	2	3	4	5	6	7	8
G score	2.4	3.0	3.7	4.6	5.6	6.6	7.7	9.1

18

One night I was on the outskirts of the city, waiting for a bus. A panhandler approached and asked for money. I reached in the pocket where I kept change. The pocket was heavy with coins. Since I was happy and feeling kindly toward the world, I emptied the contents of my pocket into the outstretched hand. Without saying a word, the old man shuffled away.

Suddenly I realized the mistake I had made. The operator of a bus was not permitted to make change. No one was allowed to ride who didn't have the exact fare of fifty cents. I called the panhandler back, told him my predicament, and asked him to return two of the quarters I had given him. He refused but offered to sell them to me for a dollar bill. I bought the quarters and said, "Be sure to spend that money on food and not drink." He replied, "Do I tell you how to spend your money?"

1. **This story takes place**   Ⓐ in the heart of a city   Ⓑ in the country   Ⓒ in a forest   Ⓓ on the edge of town
2. **A panhandler is someone who**   Ⓐ works in a pan factory   Ⓑ begs for money   Ⓒ sells pans   Ⓓ drives a bus
3. **The traveler responded with**   Ⓐ surprise   Ⓑ generosity   Ⓒ disgust   Ⓓ fear
4. **The panhandler was**   Ⓐ appreciative   Ⓑ ungrateful   Ⓒ generous   Ⓓ timid
5. **The traveler's problem was that**   Ⓐ he missed the bus   Ⓑ he needed exact change for the bus   Ⓒ he didn't have a dollar   Ⓓ he wanted all his money back
6. **The panhandler sold the quarters**   Ⓐ at a profit   Ⓑ at a loss   Ⓒ for equal change   Ⓓ to the bus driver
7. **The traveler advised the panhandler to**   Ⓐ always keep sufficient bus fare   Ⓑ buy food   Ⓒ buy drink   Ⓓ go home
8. **What was the panhandler's feeling about advice?**   Ⓐ pleasure   Ⓑ he didn't want it   Ⓒ shyness   Ⓓ gratitude

No. right	1	2	3	4	5	6	7	8
G score	3.8	4.4	5.1	5.7	6.4	7.1	7.8	8.7

Thomas Jefferson wrote the Declaration of Independence and was the third President of the United States. He was also a great architect. Monticello is the home that Thomas Jefferson built. Monticello means "little mountain" in Italian. Jefferson started building the mansion on a hill near Charlottesville, Virginia, in 1770. It is considered one of the best examples of the American classic revival style of architecture.

The building materials—stone, brick, lumber, and nails—were all prepared on the land where Monticello stands. Jefferson moved into his home with his bride in 1772 and work continued on the house for many years. Monticello was his home for fifty-six years.

The mansion was later bought by Uriah Levy and given to the people of the United States as a gift. Today, Monticello is a national shrine that is open to the public.

19

1. **Monticello is located near**   Ⓐ Washington, DC   Ⓑ Charlotte, NC   Ⓒ Williamsburg, VA   Ⓓ Charlottesville, VA
2. **Jefferson was the author of**   Ⓐ many books on architecture   Ⓑ the Constitution   Ⓒ the American Classic Revival   Ⓓ the Declaration of Independence
3. **Monticello was Jefferson's home for**   Ⓐ his whole life   Ⓑ 56 years   Ⓒ 65 years   Ⓓ summer months only
4. **In Italian, Monticello means little**   Ⓐ cello   Ⓑ house   Ⓒ mountain   Ⓓ mansion
5. **Jefferson was**   Ⓐ the first president of the U.S.   Ⓑ an Italian president   Ⓒ the 3rd American president   Ⓓ the president of Virginia
6. **Monticello is considered a fine example of**   Ⓐ a little mansion   Ⓑ American gothic revival style   Ⓒ classic Greek revival style   Ⓓ American classic revival style
7. **Jefferson moved into Monticello in**   Ⓐ 1756   Ⓑ 1770   Ⓒ 1772   Ⓓ 1776
8. **Monticello was given as a gift to the American people by**   Ⓐ the public   Ⓑ Thomas Jefferson   Ⓒ Uriah Levy   Ⓓ a national shrine

No. right	1	2	3	4	5	6	7	8
G score	3.8	4.3	5.0	5.7	6.5	7.2	7.9	8.8

20

Fall is a favorite time in Munich, Germany. In late September, a major festival begins. It is called the Oktoberfest, and it goes on into early October.

For the adults there is plenty of beer. It is served in huge tents set up in the park. For everyone there is lots of roast chicken with radishes and pretzels. The twisted pretzels come in many sizes. You can find some larger than your head.

The *Fest* begins with a parade of floats. Oom-pah bands play German folk music. The men wear short gray pants called *lederhosen*. The women wear very colorful dresses called *dirndls*.

What do the children like best? There are carnival rides! For the two weeks of the *Fest*, they can ride roller coasters, bumper cars, and many other favorites. Bright lights in all colors make the park very beautiful at night. Every visitor who has been there longs to return for another Oktoberfest.

1. **What food is larger than your head?**   Ⓐ the radishes   Ⓑ some pretzels   Ⓒ glasses of beer   Ⓓ chicken legs
2. **The *Fest* begins with**   Ⓐ the carnival rides   Ⓑ the roast chicken   Ⓒ strings of lights   Ⓓ a parade
3. **The men's short pants are called**   Ⓐ lederhosen   Ⓑ dirndls   Ⓒ overalls   Ⓓ jeans
4. **The Oktoberfest really begins in**   Ⓐ August   Ⓑ September   Ⓒ October   Ⓓ December
5. **The Oktoberfest lasts for**   Ⓐ two days   Ⓑ one week   Ⓒ two weeks   Ⓓ two months
6. **The oom-pah bands play**   Ⓐ German folk music   Ⓑ American songs   Ⓒ movie music   Ⓓ church music
7. **What do the children like best?**   Ⓐ the lederhosen   Ⓑ the radishes   Ⓒ the beer   Ⓓ the carnival rides
8. **This story is mainly about**   Ⓐ a park with tents   Ⓑ a German festival   Ⓒ carnival rides   Ⓓ large pretzels

No. right	1	2	3	4	5	6	7	8
G score	3.8	4.4	5.1	5.7	6.5	7.2	7.9	8.8

21

Talk about cats' eyes that can see in the dark! We now have something that can see when it is so dark or foggy that even a cat cannot see. With this "eye," airplane pilots can see to land their airplanes in any weather, day or night. Ships' pilots, who once were afraid to enter harbors during darkness or thick fog, now enter under these conditions without fear. This wonderful invention is called radar.

How does radar operate? Short-wave impulses, one after another, are sent out by airplane or ship. As the short waves bounce back from objects, a receiver turns them into a picture of the object they have struck. Human eyes can see this picture, and pilots watch it as they steer their ships safely through the dark and the fog.

1. **What is now used that sees better than cats' eyes?** Ⓐ radium Ⓑ radio Ⓒ radar Ⓓ an airplane
2. **Airplane pilots need radar to** Ⓐ bring ships into harbor Ⓑ land in any kind of weather Ⓒ see as well as cats Ⓓ bounce on the waves
3. **Ships' pilots now enter harbors during thick fog without** Ⓐ steering Ⓑ fear Ⓒ waves Ⓓ rolling
4. **These new "eyes" see by means of what wave impulses?** Ⓐ long Ⓑ short Ⓒ medium Ⓓ irregular
5. **How do these wave impulses behave? They** Ⓐ dance Ⓑ flutter Ⓒ float Ⓓ bounce
6. **What turns these wave impulses into pictures?** Ⓐ a camera Ⓑ an engine Ⓒ a receiver Ⓓ a ship
7. **When is the picture of an object seen? When the wave impulses are** Ⓐ leaving the ship Ⓑ nearing the object Ⓒ hitting the object Ⓓ returning from the object
8. **To see the pictures of objects pilots must** Ⓐ put on dark glasses Ⓑ use only their eyes Ⓒ use strong lenses Ⓓ use field glasses

No. right	1	2	3	4	5	6	7	8
G score	3.8	4.4	5.1	5.8	6.5	7.3	8.0	9.0

22

During the early 1970s, the U.S. Navy spent four years and $375,000 on flight tests for a strange looking object. High on a cliff in Utah, a flat, saucer-shaped object was flight tested again and again. The Navy hoped that this new device could be used to carry flares during its slow, quiet glide across the sky. What was this mysterious new military device? Flying saucers in the U.S. Navy?

Not quite. The Navy was trying to enlist the common frisbee for active duty. The same frisbee shape that has sailed over playgrounds throughout the world was at last rejected by the Navy. Chances are that the frisbee may never be used for military purposes, but they will probably continue to appear on military bases throughout the world. Don't be surprised if you see a group of servicemen tossing a frisbee high into the air—just for fun!

1. **The story says that the U.S. Navy** Ⓐ invented the frisbee Ⓑ developed flying saucers Ⓒ tested the frisbee Ⓓ shoots the frisbee from a gun
2. **The frisbee was tested for** Ⓐ ten weeks Ⓑ ten years Ⓒ four months Ⓓ four years
3. **The military use intended for the frisbee was to** Ⓐ carry flares Ⓑ carry bombs Ⓒ find enemy submarines Ⓓ provide target practice
4. **The future role of the frisbee in the U.S. Navy will be for** Ⓐ carrying flares Ⓑ recreation Ⓒ sending secret messages Ⓓ target practice
5. **The frisbee was flight tested in** Ⓐ Arizona Ⓑ California Ⓒ Utah Ⓓ Idaho
6. **Frisbees were of interest to the Navy because they** Ⓐ can carry heavy loads Ⓑ are fun Ⓒ are secret weapons Ⓓ can glide smoothly
7. **The U.S. Navy spent how much money testing the frisbee?** Ⓐ $375,000 Ⓑ $3,750 Ⓒ $37,000 Ⓓ $375.00
8. **Choose the best title:** Ⓐ A Sailor's Life Ⓑ The U.S. Navy Tests a Playground Toy Ⓒ Anchors Aweigh Ⓓ The Invention of the Frisbee

No. right	1	2	3	4	5	6	7	8
G score	4.1	4.7	5.4	6.1	6.9	7.6	8.6	9.5

I love block parties in the city. In the spring and fall at least one, and sometimes three or four, takes place every Saturday. We inform the necessary city agencies, get "no parking" signs put up, have the street closed off and washed down, and then set everything up.

We have banners, balloons, and flowers all over. All kinds of food, second-hand stuff, and arts and crafts are sold at tables. The local potters, painters, weavers, and other craftspeople give 10 percent of the money they make to the block association. There are all sorts of booths for children—face painting, knock-over-the bottles, shave-a-balloon, and fortune-telling. We have music, dancing, and entertainment. We sell plants and window boxes to beautify the street.

We make about $1000 at each party and use the money to buy trees for our streets. We pay for them and measure for the best planting spots. All the city has to do is plant the trees.

1. **Block parties take place** Ⓐ on Sunday Ⓑ in the streets Ⓒ in my house Ⓓ all year long
2. **The best months for block parties are** Ⓐ May and October Ⓑ July and August Ⓒ February and November Ⓓ December and January
3. **To get ready** Ⓐ cars are parked on the street Ⓑ three or four tables are set up Ⓒ the street is cleaned up and closed to traffic Ⓓ the mayor is invited
4. **Before the party begins, the street is** Ⓐ decorated Ⓑ painted Ⓒ planted with trees Ⓓ filled with parking signs
5. **The money we make is used to** Ⓐ buy games for children Ⓑ make the street a nicer place Ⓒ open an arts and crafts store Ⓓ pay the dancers
6. **The artists and craftspeople keep** Ⓐ all the money Ⓑ 10 per cent of the money Ⓒ most of the money Ⓓ $1000
7. **What *can't* you do in the street on the day of the party?** Ⓐ watch a show Ⓑ eat all kinds of food Ⓒ play games Ⓓ drive a car
8. **Choose the best title:** Ⓐ Getting People Together Ⓑ Music and Dancing in the City Ⓒ How to Make Money Ⓓ Planting Trees and Flowers

No. right	1	2	3	4	5	6	7	8
G score	3.8	4.4	5.1	5.8	6.5	7.3	8.1	9.1

24

The Town Council had its regular Wednesday meeting last night at 8 p.m. at Town Hall. Mrs. Watkins, the chairperson, opened the meeting.

The first topic discussed was the need to repair Wood Street. Mr. Johnson pointed out that it is filled with potholes. He added that these potholes are so deep that they are dangerous.

Mr. Perkins agreed that Wood Street is in bad shape but, he said, so are many other streets including West Street and Monroe Avenue. Mrs. Fredericks made a motion that a committee be formed to identify which streets are in the worst shape. The motion was passed, and Mrs. Fredericks was named chairperson of the committee.

The Council also discussed whether a second public swimming pool should be built this spring. Mr. Smith felt a second pool is not needed at this time. Mr. Brown agreed. Mr. Brown made a motion that a second pool not be built this year. The motion passed 4–2.

---

1. **The chairperson of the Town Council is**   Ⓐ Mrs. Fredericks   Ⓑ Mr. Smith   Ⓒ Mr. Brown   Ⓓ Mrs. Watkins
2. **Mr. Brown said that**   Ⓐ a new pool wasn't needed   Ⓑ a committee should study the pool question   Ⓒ Wood Street is in bad shape   Ⓓ Mrs. Watkins should be chairperson
3. **Mr. Perkins said that West Street is**   Ⓐ a good place for the new pool   Ⓑ in good shape   Ⓒ in bad shape   Ⓓ better than Monroe Avenue
4. **The Council voted to**   Ⓐ study the street problem   Ⓑ repair Wood Street   Ⓒ build a swimming pool   Ⓓ study the swimming pool question
5. **How many swimming pools does the town have?**   Ⓐ none   Ⓑ one   Ⓒ two   Ⓓ three
6. **This article came from which day's newspaper?**   Ⓐ Wednesday's   Ⓑ Sunday's   Ⓒ Monday's   Ⓓ Thursday's
7. **According to Mr. Johnson, Wood Street is**   Ⓐ too narrow   Ⓑ a good place for the new pool   Ⓒ dangerous   Ⓓ no worse than Monroe Avenue
8. **How many people voted against a new swimming pool?**   Ⓐ all of the council   Ⓑ only Mr. Perkins   Ⓒ four   Ⓓ two

No. right	1	2	3	4	5	6	7	8
G score	3.8	4.6	5.3	6.0	6.9	7.7	8.7	9.8

Many young people are not aware that rock and roll music has a very long and interesting history.

The "roots" of rock music can be traced all the way back through the history of black Americans.

More than a century ago, slaves at work shouted long ballads of pain and sorrow in fields throughout the South. Early in the twentieth century, W. C. Handy and others began making this music, called *the blues*, very popular. *St. Louis Blues* was one of Handy's most famous songs. This same blues style evolved into *boogie-woogie* music during the 1930s.

Blues music is still very popular today, especially in cities like Chicago where many blues singers migrated from the South. Throughout the 1960s and 1970s many songs recorded by British groups such as the Rolling Stones were based on old blues songs. Rock music, now played throughout the world, is partly a product of one of America's native art forms—the blues.

1. **The basic form of rock music can be traced to**   Ⓐ the Pilgrims   Ⓑ Spanish settlers   Ⓒ American Indians   Ⓓ black Americans
2. **Today blues music is**   Ⓐ no longer played   Ⓑ very popular in some cities   Ⓒ played only in Britain   Ⓓ used only for writing rock music
3. **According to the story, blues music is popular in Chicago because**   Ⓐ it is a large city   Ⓑ there are many concert halls   Ⓒ many blues singers moved there   Ⓓ it is a Southern city
4. **Boogie-woogie is**   Ⓐ popular music from the 1830's   Ⓑ an Indian folk dance   Ⓒ popular music from the 1930's   Ⓓ played on the violin
5. **A British group that was strongly influenced by the blues is the**   Ⓐ London Symphony   Ⓑ Beach Boys   Ⓒ Rolling Stones   Ⓓ Duke Ellington Orchestra
6. **The blues is probably considered to be a native American art form because it**   Ⓐ came from early British settlers   Ⓑ was developed by black Americans   Ⓒ came from France   Ⓓ is played around the world
7. **W. C. Handy was a composer of the**   Ⓐ early 20th century   Ⓑ 1970's   Ⓒ Civil War period   Ⓓ 1960's
8. **Choose the best title:**   Ⓐ Rock Music Was Born in the Blues   Ⓑ Meet the Rolling Stones   Ⓒ The Music of the 1940's   Ⓓ The Culture of Great Britain

No. right	1	2	3	4	5	6	7	8
G score	3.4	3.9	4.6	5.5	6.3	7.2	8.2	9.4

26

The human nervous system has two parts. There is the central nervous system and the peripheral nervous system. Peripheral means having to do with the outer part. The central nervous system is made up of the brain and the spinal cord. Everything else in the nervous system is the peripheral system.

Suppose you see a bank robber running away, down the street. The police ask you, "Which way did he go?" Your eyes already gave your brain the message, "Down the street." Your brain then sends a message along the spinal cord to the peripheral nerves in your arm. These nerves look like long pieces of thread, but they are not one continuous strand. They branch out at the end where the nerve cell is located. When the message comes along, it has to jump across these gaps. That gap is called a synapse. The message travels along, jumping synapses at regular intervals, until it reaches the terminal, or end nerve fibers. The terminal fibers are connected to the muscles. As your arm and hand muscles get the message, you point down the street where the robber is running.

1. **How many parts are there to the nervous system?**   Ⓐ 1   Ⓑ 2   Ⓒ 3   Ⓓ 4

2. **Peripheral means having to do with**   Ⓐ the body   Ⓑ the synapses   Ⓒ the outer part   Ⓓ messages

3. **The central nervous system is made up of the brain and**   Ⓐ everything else   Ⓑ the periphery   Ⓒ the spinal cord   Ⓓ the synapse

4. **All other nerves besides the central nervous system are in the**   Ⓐ brain   Ⓑ spinal cord   Ⓒ synapse   Ⓓ peripheral nervous system

5. **The gap a message jumps is called**   Ⓐ peripheral   Ⓑ a thread   Ⓒ a synapse   Ⓓ nervous

6. **The peripheral system looks**   Ⓐ grey   Ⓑ like thread   Ⓒ like the central nervous system   Ⓓ like the spinal cord

7. **The end or terminal nerve fibers are connected to**   Ⓐ gaps   Ⓑ the spinal cord   Ⓒ muscles   Ⓓ nothing

8. **Choose the best title:**   Ⓐ Which Way Did He Go?   Ⓑ The Central Nervous System   Ⓒ How the Nervous System Works   Ⓓ What Happens When We Run

The largest planet in our solar system is Jupiter. It is the fifth planet from the sun. It has a diameter of about 88,700 miles. That is nearly eleven times greater than the Earth's diameter. Its mass is about two and one half times that of all the other eight planets combined.

Nobody really knows what the surface of Jupiter looks like. It can't be seen even with powerful telescopes, because of Jupiter's atmosphere. The atmosphere on Jupiter is a heavy mixture of gases that nobody on Earth could possibly breathe. Some scientists believe there may not be any definite surface on the planet at all. They think the gases may just become more dense as they get closer to the center of the planet until they become solid.

Jupiter revolves around the sun once in just under twelve years. In spite of its size, it rotates on its axis once in just under ten hours. Unlike Earth with 365 days to a year, Jupiter has a year with about 10,512 days.

1. **Jupiter has a diameter about** Ⓐ 10 times greater than Earth's Ⓑ 2½ times greater than Earth's Ⓒ 11 times greater than Earth's Ⓓ 8 times greater than Earth's
2. **Which planet is Jupiter from the sun?** Ⓐ 3rd Ⓑ 4th Ⓒ 5th Ⓓ 6th
3. **How many planets are there in the solar system?** Ⓐ 7 Ⓑ 8 Ⓒ 9 Ⓓ 10
4. **The surface of Jupiter can be seen** Ⓐ with a powerful telescope Ⓑ by some scientists Ⓒ by no one Ⓓ with the naked eye
5. **Some scientists suspect Jupiter may have** Ⓐ no surface Ⓑ no atmosphere Ⓒ a good climate Ⓓ forms of life
6. **The atmosphere on Jupiter is made of** Ⓐ nothing Ⓑ air Ⓒ gases Ⓓ clouds
7. **The time it takes a planet to rotate on its axis once, is called a** Ⓐ month Ⓑ diameter Ⓒ day Ⓓ year
8. **When a planet revolves around the sun once, that is called** Ⓐ a light year Ⓑ ten hours Ⓒ a day Ⓓ a year

No. right	1	2	3	4	5	6	7	8
G score	4.0	4.6	5.3	6.1	6.9	7.7	8.6	9.6

28

On a night in May during World War II, one of the finest battle-ships ever built—the *Bismarck*—put out to sea to fight the British. Britain's largest battle cruiser, the *Hood*, and one of her best battle-ships, the *Prince of Wales*, gave battle.

The *Bismarck's* second salvo injured the *Prince of Wales*, which dropped out of the running fight. The third salvo broke the *Hood* in two, and while the two halves sank, officers and men of the *Bismarck* cheered and sang and danced on deck. The "unsinkable" *Bismarck* sailed on, looking for new conquests.

Then one morning the men on the *Bismarck* learned that the hunter was being hunted. An American-made seaplane appeared through an opening in the clouds. After that wherever the *Bismarck* went, eyes were watching from the sky.

1. **"One of the finest battleships ever built" was the**　Ⓐ *Hood*
   Ⓑ *Arizona*　Ⓒ *Prince of Wales*　Ⓓ *Bismarck*
2. **The *Hood* belonged to**　Ⓐ England　Ⓑ France　Ⓒ Germany
   Ⓓ Italy
3. **The *Prince of Wales* was a**　Ⓐ destroyer　Ⓑ cruiser　Ⓒ battleship
   Ⓓ submarine
4. **The British battle cruiser was**　Ⓐ torpedoed　Ⓑ injured　Ⓒ broken
   in two　Ⓓ not hit
5. **When the *Hood* sank, the men on the *Bismarck* were**　Ⓐ happy
   Ⓑ sad　Ⓒ cross　Ⓓ silent
6. **What was hunting the *Bismarck*? A**　Ⓐ battleship　Ⓑ cruiser
   Ⓒ seaplane　Ⓓ fortress
7. **The eyes watching the *Bismarck* belonged to**　Ⓐ the crew of the
   battleship　Ⓑ those in the seaplane　Ⓒ English officers　Ⓓ no one
   knows who
8. **The *Bismarck* was looking for**　Ⓐ other ships to sink　Ⓑ eyes in the
   sky　Ⓒ an opening in the clouds　Ⓓ an unsinkable British ship

No. right	1	2	3	4	5	6	7	8
G score	3.5	4.0	4.7	5.6	6.5	7.3	8.3	9.4

A flight of British Swordfish planes came roaring out of the clouds. One of their torpedoes exploded against the side of the *Bismarck*. That night the planes sent three more torpedoes crashing against the ship. One damaged the rudder, causing the ship to travel in circles. About midnight, as the *Bismarck* circled, a pack of British destroyers surrounded the battleship, sending more torpedoes into her.

In the morning the battleships *Rodney* and *George V* arrived and began pounding the wounded *Bismarck* with their great 16-inch guns at a distance of eleven miles. They moved in closer and closer, until the range was only two miles. The *Bismarck* fought back. She seemed unsinkable, and her men would not surrender. Never before had a ship taken such punishment and remained afloat. At last, her flag still flying, the bow went up, the stern went down, and the pride of the German navy slid under the waves, taking her crew with her.

1. **How many torpedoes hit the *Bismarck* before midnight?** Ⓐ one Ⓑ two Ⓒ three Ⓓ four
2. **How many destroyers attacked the ship after midnight?** Ⓐ a pack Ⓑ three Ⓒ a flight Ⓓ a few
3. **British Swordfish fight** Ⓐ from the water Ⓑ from the air Ⓒ on the ground Ⓓ under the water
4. **The *Bismarck* was forced to travel in circles because of injury to her** Ⓐ deck Ⓑ sides Ⓒ engines Ⓓ rudder
5. **Destroyers attacked the battleship from** Ⓐ all sides Ⓑ one side Ⓒ in front Ⓓ its rear
6. **The *Bismarck*** Ⓐ surrendered Ⓑ wounded the *Rodney* Ⓒ fired 16-inch guns Ⓓ sank
7. **The "pride of the German navy" was the** Ⓐ *Hood* Ⓑ *Bismarck* Ⓒ *George V* Ⓓ *Rodney*
8. **The crew of the sunken ship was** Ⓐ American Ⓑ English Ⓒ German Ⓓ French

No. right	1	2	3	4	5	6	7	8
G score	3.7	4.4	5.2	6.0	6.9	7.7	8.8	9.9

STRAWBERRY BREAD

30

Ingredients:

1 pint strawberries
1 3/4 cups sifted flour
¼ teaspoon baking soda
½ teaspoon salt

1/3 cup shortening
2/3 cup sugar
2 eggs, well beaten

Wash and hull the strawberries, pat them dry, and mash them up or purée them in a blender. Sift together the dry ingredients. Cream the shortening and add the sugar gradually until it's light and fluffy. Add the eggs and beat well. Add the flour mixture alternately with 1 cup of strawberry purée and beat until smooth. Turn the mixture into a well-greased loaf pan and bake in a pre-heated 350° oven for 1 hour and 10 minutes or until a toothpick inserted into the center comes out clean.

1. **Which of these is *not* a dry ingredient?** Ⓐ flour Ⓑ baking soda Ⓒ salt Ⓓ eggs
2. **The sugar should be** Ⓐ added a little at a time Ⓑ well beaten Ⓒ puréed in a blender Ⓓ sifted with the shortening
3. **The shortening should be** Ⓐ mixed with the flour until smooth Ⓑ creamed with the sugar until light and fluffy Ⓒ beaten with the eggs until dry Ⓓ puréed with the salt until clean
4. **You will need a teaspoon to measure** Ⓐ the eggs Ⓑ the flour Ⓒ the salt Ⓓ the shortening
5. **Measure the flour with a** Ⓐ cup Ⓑ pint Ⓒ teaspoon Ⓓ blender
6. **The oven should be** Ⓐ heated before you put the pan in Ⓑ on for ten hours Ⓒ well greased Ⓓ inserted with a toothpick
7. **Put the mixture in** Ⓐ a pre-heated blender Ⓑ a loaf pan Ⓒ a bread box Ⓓ a well-greased cup
8. **The bread is done** Ⓐ when the oven reaches 350° Ⓑ after an hour and a half is up Ⓒ when a toothpick poked into it comes out clean Ⓓ after 10 minutes

No. right	1	2	3	4	5	6	7	8
G score	3.8	4.6	5.3	6.0	7.0	7.8	8.8	9.9

The city of Portland, Oregon, had nothing but trouble with its new fireboat. The city paid $147,889 for it. First, it was delivered later than had been promised. Then the people in Portland found out that it had not been built exactly according to the plans. It had to be sent back to a factory in San Diego to be fixed and have parts rebuilt. When these repairs were made, the boat could not be shipped directly but had to be sent all the way around through Mexico, Arizona, and Nevada.

Then the engines proved to be faulty. Finally they, too, were replaced. Portland's fire department took the new fireboat into the Willamette River for another trial.

It sank.

1. **Portland's new boat was** Ⓐ ill-fated Ⓑ promptly delivered Ⓒ made in Mexico Ⓓ according to plan

2. **How much did it cost to buy?** Ⓐ a little over fourteen thousand dollars Ⓑ almost one hundred and fifty thousand dollars Ⓒ almost one and half million dollars Ⓓ about a hundred and forty seven dollars

3. **The fireboat had to be** Ⓐ changed to fit the plans Ⓑ replaced in San Diego Ⓒ delivered to Nevada Ⓓ fixed in Oregon

4. **The boat was sent back to Portland** Ⓐ directly Ⓑ over the water Ⓒ by going south and then east and then north Ⓓ from San Diego through the Willamette River.

5. **The engines were** Ⓐ not functioning perfectly Ⓑ on fire Ⓒ built according to plan Ⓓ made in Arizona

6. **The engines later** Ⓐ were fixed Ⓑ were shipped Ⓒ were painted Ⓓ were replaced

7. **The last test of the boat was** Ⓐ a success Ⓑ a failure Ⓒ in the fire department Ⓓ at a factory in San Diego

8. **Choose the best title:** Ⓐ Portland's Fire Department Ⓑ Trouble in San Diego Ⓒ The Little Fireboat that Wouldn't Ⓓ The Willamette River Showboat

No. right	1	2	3	4	5	6	7	8
G score	4.0	4.6	5.4	6.2	7.1	7.9	8.9	9.9

32

There is a small group whose job it is to fly a plane into hurricanes. Recently they flew a plane into a hurricane with winds blowing 115 miles an hour. Had the plane been anchored to the ground, the winds would have torn it to bits. Inside the hurricane, the plane shook, rocked, and bucked, and the wings bent far beyond what was thought possible.

The ocean roared only 100 feet beneath the plane, but it was difficult for the men inside to see the water because rain lashed every window. No doubt there were giant waves, but all that could be seen below was a smooth sheet of flying water. No one bothered to put on a life jacket. If the plane went down, nothing could live in such waters.

Radio messages were sent from the plane, but none could be received by it. Static was so loud that earphones could not be worn without injury to the fliers' ears.

At last the plane passed through one side of the hurricane and entered the quiet sunlit eye in its center. The pilot circled this eye and then flew the plane safely back through the storm toward home.

---

1. **What happened to the pilot?** Ⓐ he completed his mission successfully Ⓑ his eye was injured Ⓒ he saw his home in the sunlight Ⓓ he flew at 115 miles per hour
2. **When flying inside the hurricane, all that could be seen below was** Ⓐ a smooth sheet of water Ⓑ heavy mist Ⓒ angry waves Ⓓ nothing
3. **It was difficult to see out because** Ⓐ the windows were dirty Ⓑ there were no windows Ⓒ there were no windshield wipers Ⓓ rain lashed every window
4. **Parts of the plane itself were** Ⓐ flexible Ⓑ inflexible Ⓒ fragile Ⓓ made of rigid iron
5. **The fliers did not use life jackets because** Ⓐ nothing could live in the water below Ⓑ they had none Ⓒ they were clumsy to wear Ⓓ it was raining
6. **Radio messages were** Ⓐ sent from the plane Ⓑ received Ⓒ not heard Ⓓ not sent
7. **No radio messages were received because** Ⓐ there were no earphones Ⓑ no one knew how to operate earphones Ⓒ static was too loud Ⓓ none were sent
8. **The center of the hurricane was** Ⓐ 100 feet below the plane Ⓑ tranquil Ⓒ tearing the plane to bits Ⓓ hurting the fliers' ears

No. right	1	2	3	4	5	6	7	8
G score	3.7	4.3	5.1	6.0	6.9	7.8	8.9	10.0

There were about 300,000 blind termites or white ants in a termite nest. About 100,000 of them grew wings, left the darkness they loved, sought the light, and flew away in many directions. A male and a female came to earth together. They lost their wings, found a crack in a rotten log or plank, and mated. The male soon died, but the female lived on for ten, twenty, thirty, or more years.

The female began a new colony, laying eggs that hatched out sexless worker and warrior ants. This queen laid many thousand eggs a day, perhaps 100,000,000 eggs during her lifetime.

These millions of termites, eating damp wood, cause damage to houses and other buildings amounting to millions of dollars every year. There are certain simple rules to be followed in guarding against destruction caused by termites. No wooden part of a building should touch the ground. The supports for a building should be of stone, concrete, or similar material. Painting wood nearest the ground with creosote is an added caution. Do not build your house so that it may become a home for termites!

1. **How many of the termites in the nest grew wings?** Ⓐ one-quarter Ⓑ one-third Ⓒ one-half Ⓓ all
2. **All the termites that grew wings flew away in** Ⓐ the same direction Ⓑ opposite directions Ⓒ many directions Ⓓ four directions
3. **After mating, the female died** Ⓐ at once Ⓑ soon Ⓒ in two years Ⓓ after many years
4. **The termite that lived a long time was called a** Ⓐ king Ⓑ female Ⓒ queen Ⓓ male
5. **These insects love to eat** Ⓐ dry wood Ⓑ damp wood Ⓒ hard wood Ⓓ any kind of wood
6. **The wooden parts of a building should** Ⓐ reach bedrock Ⓑ go deep into the ground Ⓒ not touch the ground Ⓓ support the building
7. **What may termites do to our houses?** Ⓐ build them Ⓑ cover them Ⓒ strengthen them Ⓓ weaken them
8. **The function of creosoting is to** Ⓐ minimize destruction Ⓑ facilitate mating Ⓒ cover stone and concrete Ⓓ multiply males

No. right	1	2	3	4	5	6	7	8
G score	4.1	4.7	5.5	6.3	7.1	7.9	8.9	9.9

34

As we travel from coast to coast we are likely to think what a very large world this is in which we live. Still, to the astronomer, the earth is one of the small planets—in fact, its diameter is less than one-eleventh the diameter of the largest planet, Jupiter. Even Jupiter, however, is small in comparison with the sun, whose diameter is ten times as great as Jupiter's. How insignificant the earth is, then, in comparison with our sun!

As you look at the sun in the western sky in the early evening, do you ever think how far away it is? One could travel around the earth three thousand times and still not travel as far as the sun is from the earth. Light, traveling at the rate of 186,000 miles per second, requires eight and one-third minutes to pass from the sun to the earth.

1. **An astronomer is someone who** Ⓐ travels coast to coast   Ⓑ studies the planets   Ⓒ comes from Jupiter   Ⓓ travels around the earth
2. **Among planets, the earth is** Ⓐ large   Ⓑ medium-sized   Ⓒ largest   Ⓓ small
3. **About how many times larger is Jupiter's diameter than the earth's?** Ⓐ 10   Ⓑ 11   Ⓒ 70   Ⓓ 110
4. **How big is Jupiter compared to the sun?** Ⓐ one-tenth as big   Ⓑ eight and a third times larger   Ⓒ three thousand times bigger   Ⓓ 186,000 miles smaller
5. **In the evening, the sun is** Ⓐ in the western sky   Ⓑ near Jupiter   Ⓒ traveling around the earth   Ⓓ 3000 miles away
6. **Light travels at the rate of** Ⓐ 186,000 miles per second   Ⓑ 50,250 miles per hour   Ⓒ 186,000 miles per hour   Ⓓ eight and one-third miles per minute
7. **It takes 8⅓ minutes for** Ⓐ the earth to go around the sun   Ⓑ Jupiter to go around the earth   Ⓒ light to travel from earth to the sun   Ⓓ light to go from the sun to earth
8. **The distance of the earth from the sun is** Ⓐ more than 3000 trips around the earth   Ⓑ less than from coast to coast   Ⓒ ten times the earth's diameter   Ⓓ as far as it is to Jupiter

No. right	1	2	3	4	5	6	7	8
G score	4.0	4.6	5.5	6.2	7.1	7.9	9.0	10.0

Help Wanted

Automobile Mechanic's Assistant. Well-known local gas station. 1–2 year's experience desirable but not necessary. 40-hour week. Some overtime and Saturday work. Must have driver's license and references. Starting $3.75/hour. 2-weeks paid vacation. Call for appointment. 887-6263. Harry's Employment Agency.

1. **The person who wrote this ad wants to find** Ⓐ an experienced mechanic Ⓑ somebody to pump gas Ⓒ somebody to drive a truck Ⓓ a mechanic's helper

2. **To get this job you have to** Ⓐ have at least one year's experience Ⓑ have a driver's license Ⓒ be willing to work on Sundays Ⓓ have a high school diploma

3. **You could not take this job if you** Ⓐ were unable to work on a weekend Ⓑ have never worked on cars Ⓒ were a girl Ⓓ wear glasses

4. **The person who gets this job should count on** Ⓐ working no more than 40 hours per week Ⓑ spending a lot of time at the agency Ⓒ becoming the gas station manager Ⓓ working more than 40 hours some weeks

5. **To learn more about this job you should** Ⓐ call the gas station Ⓑ call the employment agency Ⓒ go visit the employment agency Ⓓ call the newspaper

6. **The pay offered for this job is** Ⓐ $3.75 per day Ⓑ $40 per week Ⓒ $3.75 per hour to start Ⓓ $3.75 per hour after one year

7. **You will get a two-week vacation** Ⓐ without pay Ⓑ after working a 40-hour week Ⓒ when you make an appointment Ⓓ at regular pay

8. **If you got this job, you would work at** Ⓐ the newspaper Ⓑ Harry's Employment Agency Ⓒ a local gas station Ⓓ the city garage

No. right	1	2	3	4	5	6	7	8
G score	4.0	4.7	5.6	6.5	7.4	8.4	9.5	10.5

36

Solder is a very useful metal. It is made of a mixture of tin and lead. It can be used to join or connect small metal objects. For example, it is used to connect pieces of copper tubing. It is also used to connect electrical wires.

No matter what you plan to solder, there are several rules you must follow to do a good job.

First, the surfaces to be soldered must be shiny clean. No dirt. No paint. No grease. No rust.

Second, soldering paste should be used. This will help the solder stick.

Third, and most important, the solder should not be melted by the direct heat of the blow torch or soldering iron. Instead, whatever is being soldered should be heated. Then, the solder should be touched to the surfaces to be joined. The solder should be melted by the hot surfaces rather than by the iron or torch. If you try to solder without heating the surfaces the solder may not stick.

1. **Solder is made of a mixture of** Ⓐ copper and lead Ⓑ tin and lead Ⓒ tin and copper Ⓓ lead and iron
2. **Solder can be used to connect** Ⓐ small metal objects Ⓑ metal and plastic Ⓒ any metal objects Ⓓ metal and glass
3. **The surfaces to be soldered must be** Ⓐ new Ⓑ clean Ⓒ flat Ⓓ soft
4. **Soldering paste is used** Ⓐ to clean the soldering iron Ⓑ only when soldering copper tubing Ⓒ to hold the metal surfaces together Ⓓ to help the solder stick
5. **How many rules does the author give?** Ⓐ six Ⓑ four Ⓒ three Ⓓ five
6. **A soldering iron is used to** Ⓐ smooth the surfaces to be soldered Ⓑ clean the surfaces to be soldered Ⓒ melt the solder Ⓓ heat the surfaces to be soldered
7. **The solder should be melted** Ⓐ by a blow torch Ⓑ before starting to solder Ⓒ by the surfaces to be joined Ⓓ in a special pot
8. **According to the author, if you do not follow the rules** Ⓐ you will hurt yourself Ⓑ you will not do a good job Ⓒ you will only be able to solder small objects Ⓓ you will have to use a blow torch

No. right	1	2	3	4	5	6	7	8
G score	4.4	5.1	5.8	6.5	7.3	8.1	9.2	10.0

It may resemble a drum, a banana, or an acorn. It can be shaped like a turban, heart, bell, or remain flat. Its edges are sometimes scalloped. Some are squat, some are oblong, and others have thick, swollen bodies. Their necks can be long, thin, short, straight, or crooked.

Their size may be as small as your hand or they may weigh up to 100 to 150 pounds. Their skins can be smooth, furrowed, wrinkled, or warty. Most of them are in shades of green, but many have yellow, silver, or black overtones. They also come in white, cream color, buff, tan, pink, blue, orange, and in bright yellow and red-golds.

They have names such as Hungarian mammoth, scallopini, gold nugget, buttercup, patty pan, crookneck, black jack, goldzini, cocozelle, big red, blue banana, kikuzu, Chicago warted hubbard, umatilla marblehead, and ponca.

Are these fantastic figures from a book of fairy tales or science fiction? No, they are just varieties of a vegetable that has been enjoyed since as long ago as 5000 B.C.—squash.

1. **Squash is** Ⓐ a monster Ⓑ something to eat Ⓒ a fantastic science fiction creature Ⓓ a very large Hungarian
2. **Their most common color is** Ⓐ red-gold Ⓑ white Ⓒ silver and black Ⓓ green
3. **Some varieties are shaped like** Ⓐ flowers Ⓑ hands Ⓒ overtones Ⓓ a kind of hat
4. **Some squash can weigh as much as** Ⓐ a mammoth Ⓑ an average woman Ⓒ a feather Ⓓ 5000 lbs
5. **The edges sometimes** Ⓐ have sharp, pointy tips Ⓑ have gold nuggets Ⓒ taste like bananas Ⓓ are shaped like sea-shells
6. **Which one of these would be a very big squash?** Ⓐ kikuza Ⓑ Chicago warted hubbard Ⓒ buttercup Ⓓ Hungarian mammoth
7. **Their skins can be** Ⓐ like fur Ⓑ bumpy Ⓒ made of silver and gold Ⓓ slimy
8. **We know that squash has been a food** Ⓐ for about 70 centuries Ⓑ in fairy tales Ⓒ for upwards of 100 to 150 years Ⓓ for people who want to grow big

No. right	1	2	3	4	5	6	7	8
G score	5.9	6.6	7.2	7.7	8.4	9.2	9.9	10.6

38

How do we measure the distance of stars? We say that they are "light-years" away. If a star is ten light-years away, it takes ten years for the light of the star to travel to the earth so we can see it. Light travels incredibly fast, at the rate of 186,000 miles per second.

When you look at a star, you are not seeing it as it twinkles now. You are seeing an event that took place in the past.

The star named Pollux is thirty-five light-years away. You are seeing the light it gave off thirty-five years ago! The star named Rigel is 650 light-years away. The light you see began to travel in the Middle Ages.

If a new star is born as far away as Rigel, no one will see its light for another 650 years.

Stars do die. Not all the stars we see may still be burning. If Pollux were to die tomorrow, you would still see its light in the sky for thirty-five more years.

1. **How fast does light travel?** Ⓐ 186,000 miles per hour Ⓑ 186,000 miles per second Ⓒ 186,000 miles per year Ⓓ 186,000 miles per minute
2. **If a star is ten light-years away, its light will reach the earth** Ⓐ in 35 years Ⓑ in 650 years Ⓒ in 10 years Ⓓ in 10 days
3. **We use light-years to measure** Ⓐ the heat of stars Ⓑ the size of stars Ⓒ the weight of stars Ⓓ the distance of stars
4. **A star that is 35 light-years away is** Ⓐ Pollux Ⓑ Rigel Ⓒ the sun Ⓓ Sirius
5. **The light you see from Rigel began to travel** Ⓐ in ancient times Ⓑ ten years ago Ⓒ in the Middle Ages Ⓓ last year
6. **Rigel is** Ⓐ 35 light-years away Ⓑ 35 miles away Ⓒ 650 light-years away Ⓓ 650 miles away
7. **If Pollux died tomorrow, you would see its light** Ⓐ until tomorrow Ⓑ until next week Ⓒ for another year Ⓓ for 35 more years
8. **When you see a star twinkle, you are seeing** Ⓐ an event as it takes place now Ⓑ an event that took place in the past Ⓒ an event as it will take place tomorrow Ⓓ the death of a star

No. right	1	2	3	4	5	6	7	8
G score	4.3	5.0	5.7	6.5	7.3	8.2	9.2	10.2

Not many years ago, a young girl dreamed of becoming a ballerina. Aware of her talent, she knew she would have to submit to rigorous practice and discipline. She worked faithfully. Her efforts paid off. Eventually she became a professional dancer and a famous one.

At that time, Russia was most highly regarded for ballet. Often American dancers changed their names to Russian-sounding ones, but Maria Tallchief chose to be different. Daughter of an American Indian, she was proud to be known by her native American name.

Since then, American dancers have brought more than their names to the dance. Following the example of modern dance, ballet now reflects the manifold styles and movements of ethnic groups in America. Through such artists as Alvin Ailey, José Limon, Martha Graham, and others, the vibrant cultures and experiences of black, Hispanic, Appalachian, and many other Americans have created an art form unique in content and diversity. Russia no longer sets the trends in dance.

1. **Maria Tallchief's dream required all except**   Ⓐ talent   Ⓑ discipline   Ⓒ rigorous practice   Ⓓ a Russian name
2. **The selection implies that Russia is**   Ⓐ still setting the trends   Ⓑ where Maria Tallchief studied   Ⓒ no longer the leader in dance   Ⓓ no longer training dancers
3. **Why did dancers want Russian names?**   Ⓐ they were Indians   Ⓑ they wanted to dance in Russia   Ⓒ they thought it would help their careers   Ⓓ it would be good discipline
4. **What does the selection tell us?**   Ⓐ there has been change in American dance   Ⓑ there has been no change in American dance   Ⓒ Russian dance is changing   Ⓓ ballet has always reflected American ethnicity
5. **What is the writer's attitude toward cultural diversity in dance?**   Ⓐ prefers Russian dominance   Ⓑ favors it greatly   Ⓒ disapproves   Ⓓ takes it for granted
6. **The dancer of native American background is**   Ⓐ Martha Graham   Ⓑ Maria Tallchief   Ⓒ José Limon   Ⓓ Alvin Ailey
7. **"Ethnic groups" in paragraph 3 refers to**   Ⓐ different cultural groups   Ⓑ being Indian   Ⓒ being something other than American   Ⓓ being Hispanic
8. **A useful stem word for understanding "manifold" would be**   Ⓐ fold   Ⓑ man   Ⓒ many   Ⓓ manic

No. right	1	2	3	4	5	6	7	8
G score	5.2	5.9	6.6	7.3	8.1	9.0	9.9	10.7

40

A beautiful island lies off the coast of Maine. Every summer more than thirty thousand vacationers come to Mount Desert Island to enjoy its mountains, lakes, and rocky beaches. Not many people know about the crucially important work that is done here throughout the year.

Mount Desert Island is the home of the Jackson Laboratory. Year round a staff of thirty-five scientists studies cancer, diabetes, muscular dystrophy, and many other dreaded diseases and biological problems. Since 1929, these dedicated men and women, working with many assistants, base their research on the questions of how to cure and prevent these sicknesses. Seven hundred thousand mice, bred at the laboratory, help them find the answers.

How do cancer viruses operate? Is there a connection between our diet and cancer? Is there immunity to cancer, and what could this mean? These questions illustrate some of the recent concerns of the researchers.

In addition, the laboratory inspires high school and college students each summer through a special training program for them. Though preventions and cures may seem distressingly far off, the ongoing efforts of the Jackson Laboratory give us much hope.

---

1. **The main concern of the Jackson Laboratory is** Ⓐ nutrition Ⓑ animal breeding Ⓒ marine biology Ⓓ diseases
2. **Mount Desert Island is known mainly as** Ⓐ a research center Ⓑ a health spa Ⓒ a summer vacation spot Ⓓ a riding resort
3. **Which are not found on Mount Desert Island?** Ⓐ rocky beaches Ⓑ tropical forests Ⓒ mountains Ⓓ lakes
4. **The laboratory is** Ⓐ on a mountain Ⓑ in a desert Ⓒ on an island Ⓓ open only in the summer
5. **Seven hundred thousand mice** Ⓐ plague vacationers Ⓑ live in the mountains Ⓒ cause disease Ⓓ are used in research
6. **Researchers must be** Ⓐ dedicated Ⓑ men only Ⓒ women only Ⓓ former patients
7. **Which of the following is implied?** Ⓐ in 1929, there was a staff changeover at the laboratory Ⓑ in 1929, the research procedures were changed Ⓒ in 1929, the laboratory was opened Ⓓ in 1929, the laboratory was dedicated
8. **Which of the following is not mentioned as a function of the laboratory?** Ⓐ studying cancer viruses Ⓑ training students in the summer Ⓒ breeding mice for laboratory use Ⓓ treating patients

No. right	1	2	3	4	5	6	7	8
G score	4.7	5.5	6.2	7.0	7.7	8.7	9.6	10.4

Some people still believe in vampires. A vampire is a dead body that comes to life at night. It needs fresh blood to stay alive. It gets blood by biting the neck of a sleeping victim. It does not drink all the person's blood all at once. It comes back night after night. At last, the victim dies. Then the victim becomes a vampire, too.

Vampire stories come from many parts of the world, but most stories come from eastern Europe. The most famous vampire was Count Dracula. Count Dracula was not real. He was a character in a story by Bram Stoker, but he was based on a real man named Vlad Tepes.

Vlad Tepes was a prince in the 1500s. He ruled a land called Transylvania in eastern Europe. He was not a vampire, but he was an evil man who killed his enemies by putting stakes through them. His subjects called him Dracula which means "son of the devil."

Because vampires are evil, they are frightened by anything holy. They also do not like garlic or sunlight. There is only one way to kill a vampire. You must find him in his coffin, and you must drive a stake through his heart.

1. **Choose the best title:** Ⓐ The Vampire Bat Ⓑ A Horror Story Ⓒ Vampires Ⓓ Vampires I Have Known
2. **A vampire is a** Ⓐ group of countries Ⓑ dead body that comes to life at night Ⓒ prince Ⓓ word that means "son of the devil"
3. **From the description, a vampire is most like a** Ⓐ prince Ⓑ ape Ⓒ dragon Ⓓ monster
4. **Most vampire stories come from** Ⓐ western Europe Ⓑ Asia Ⓒ England Ⓓ eastern Europe
5. **After the victim dies, it** Ⓐ rests in peace Ⓑ becomes a vampire Ⓒ becomes Count Dracula Ⓓ haunts Count Dracula
6. **Vlad Tepes was** Ⓐ not a vampire Ⓑ a king of eastern Europe Ⓒ the first vampire Ⓓ a prince of western Europe
7. **Dracula means** Ⓐ son of the devil Ⓑ vampire Ⓒ son of a bat Ⓓ prince of darkness
8. **A vampire would be afraid of** Ⓐ the sun Ⓑ an onion Ⓒ blood Ⓓ a coffin

No. right	1	2	3	4	5	6	7	8
G score	2.9	3.7	4.6	5.7	6.9	8.0	9.5	10.8

42

In the 1970s, women in sports made a name for themselves, and women's athletics began to be taken seriously. In 1973, in what was called The Battle of the Sexes, Billie Jean King beat Bobbie Riggs 6–4, 6–3, 6–3 in a winner-take-all tennis match. Said Riggs, "She was too good. She played too well." A less well known accomplishment was that of Cheryl White, who at the age of 17, in 1971, became the first black woman jockey to win a horse race. In 1975, Junko Tabei became the first woman to conquer the peak of Mt. Everest. She led a team of fifteen Japanese women. She herself was 35 years old, barely 5 feet tall, 95 pounds, and the mother of a 3-year-old when she made the historic climb. Sixty-four years earlier, another woman made mountain climbing history. She was Annie Smith Peck, who became the first person to climb Mt. Coropuna—21,250 feet—and she did it at the age of 61. She crowned the mountain with a **Votes for Women** banner.

1. **The Battle of the Sexes was between**   Ⓐ a man and a woman tennis player   Ⓑ a male and a female jockey   Ⓒ the first black mountaineers   Ⓓ Billie Jean King and Annie Smith Peck
2. **Cheryl White won the race**   Ⓐ 6-4, 6-3, 6-3   Ⓑ when she was seventeen   Ⓒ in 1917   Ⓓ when she was 5 feet tall and 95 pounds
3. **Billie Jean King won the tennis match because**   Ⓐ the winner takes all   Ⓑ she led a team of women   Ⓒ she won 4 out of 6 games   Ⓓ she played better than Riggs in all three sets
4. **Ms. Tabei was the first woman**   Ⓐ to climb Mt. Coropuna   Ⓑ to win a horse race   Ⓒ to reach the peak of Mt. Everest   Ⓓ to conquer a mountain when she was a mother
5. **When did Ms. Peck make her climb?**   Ⓐ in 1975   Ⓑ in 1964   Ⓒ in 1911   Ⓓ in 1935
6. **Annie Smith Peck was**   Ⓐ the first woman to climb Mt. Everest   Ⓑ the first person to climb Mt. Coropuna   Ⓒ the first Japanese to climb Mt. Coropuna   Ⓓ 64 years old when she climbed Mt. Coropuna
7. **Why did Ms. Peck make her climb?**   Ⓐ to lead a team of women   Ⓑ to be the oldest person to reach 21,250 ft.   Ⓒ to help women win their right to vote   Ⓓ to be crowned and given a banner at the top
8. **Women's sports are now**   Ⓐ more respected   Ⓑ lesser known   Ⓒ 3 years old   Ⓓ all played against men

No. right	1	2	3	4	5	6	7	8
G score	4.7	5.5	6.2	7.0	7.7	8.7	9.6	10.4

Few of us realize what a vast amount of information has been gathered about our feathered friends, the birds. Birds are very valuable because they destroy insects harmful to agriculture, because they feed on the seeds of weeds, and because some of them eat mice that might feed on the farmer's crops. A scarlet tanager has been known to eat six hundred and thirty caterpillars in eighteen minutes, and one nighthawk that was killed had recently eaten sixty grasshoppers, and another five hundred mosquitoes. We can estimate the vast quantity of insects that birds consume when we know that a pair of chickadees were found to have fed their young forty times in thirty minutes.

Some migratory birds, the golden plover for example, fly from Labrador or Nova Scotia to South America over the Atlantic Ocean without stopping once.

Are you surprised to know there are between thirteen and fourteen thousand species of birds in the world?

43

1. **This selection states that birds are** Ⓐ valuable to agriculture Ⓑ poisonous to man Ⓒ harmful to agriculture Ⓓ poisonous to animals
2. **Birds help the farmer by** Ⓐ helping control information Ⓑ keeping down the growth of weeds Ⓒ killing nighthawks Ⓓ migrating
3. **The bird known to have eaten over six hundred caterpillars is the** Ⓐ golden plover Ⓑ scarlet tanager Ⓒ chickadee Ⓓ nighthawk
4. **A nighthawk is reported to have contained** Ⓐ sixty grasshoppers Ⓑ vast numbers of grasshoppers Ⓒ many field mice Ⓓ 500 chickadees
5. **The golden plover can fly from Labrador to South America** Ⓐ with a short rest Ⓑ without stopping once Ⓒ with no long rest Ⓓ after four hours of rest
6. **A pair of chickadees** Ⓐ fed forty young Ⓑ took thirty minutes to find food for themselves Ⓒ fed their young forty times in half an hour Ⓓ ate thirty caterpillars
7. **Birds that fly from Labrador to South America are all called** Ⓐ plowers Ⓑ migratory Ⓒ Nova Scotia Ⓓ Atlantic
8. **The number of species of birds in the world is found to be** Ⓐ millions Ⓑ 630 Ⓒ impossible to estimate Ⓓ thousands

No. right	1	2	3	4	5	6	7	8
G score	4.6	5.3	6.1	7.0	7.8	8.8	9.9	10.8

44

Do you know the name of the man who liberated much of South America?

When he was in his early twenties, he kneeled on the Holy Mount above Rome and exclaimed, "I swear by the God of my fathers and by my native land that my hands shall never tire nor my soul rest until I have broken the chains which bind us to Spain."

Armed with this dream, he returned to South America, raised armies, and fought hundreds of battles. Each of his greatest victories set a different nation free. He was the founder of the republics of Venezuela, Colombia, Ecuador, Peru, and Bolivia. As the young conqueror entered the capital of his own country of Venezuela when it had been freed, twelve maidens dressed in white pulled his chariot with silken ropes. After his death, which occurred when he was still young, he entered his capital again, this time under mourning arches and shadowed by the flags of many nations. The name of South America's man of glory is Simón Bolívar.

1. **The hero you have just read about came from** Ⓐ Spain Ⓑ North America Ⓒ South America Ⓓ Rome
2. **Which country ruled most of South America?** Ⓐ Peru Ⓑ Venezuela Ⓒ Spain Ⓓ Bolivia
3. **Bolívar's own country was** Ⓐ Ecuador Ⓑ Colombia Ⓒ Holy Mount Ⓓ Venezuela
4. **What did the young man swear?** Ⓐ to ride a chariot Ⓑ to bind himself to Spain Ⓒ to free his father Ⓓ to free his country
5. **How many maidens pulled the chariot?** Ⓐ 10 Ⓑ 12 Ⓒ 21 Ⓓ 22
6. **Bolívar died** Ⓐ when he entered his capital Ⓑ young Ⓒ under an arch Ⓓ in Bolivia
7. **When Bolívar died, people** Ⓐ pulled his chariot Ⓑ waved flags and cheered Ⓒ grieved Ⓓ fought in the morning
8. **Choose the best title:** Ⓐ Fighting Battles Ⓑ The Great Liberator of South America Ⓒ The Man Who Conquered Spain Ⓓ A War Story

No. right	1	2	3	4	5	6	7	8
G score	4.8	5.6	6.3	7.1	7.8	8.8	9.8	10.6

All aboard a bathyscaphe for the bottom of the ocean!

Absolute darkness begins at 1300 feet down. A searchlight shows millions of small particles—living and dead. The living particles look like snowflakes, snowing upward, but the dead particles slowly settle toward the bottom. Shrimp flock to the light like moths to a flame. Many strange creatures are seen. Some are shaped like eggs strung together; some are the size and shape of a football; some are hatchet-fish, their undersides glowing like torches. At a depth of 2000 to 2500 feet, long, slender, brilliant creatures swim or stand on their heads or tails. In groups, they look like spears of growing asparagus.

On one trip, the bathyscaphe came to rest on the edge of a cliff 6000 feet below the surface. Nearby a benthosaurus used three long fins as legs on which to stand. If the bathyscaphe went down deeper it might get caught under the cliff or be wedged between canyon walls, but over and down it went.

Nearly three miles down, a small shark with great globes for eyes came into view. Near-sounding echoes proved that the bottom of the sea was not far below.

45

1. **This story tells us the bathyscaphe is used to study**   Ⓐ mud   Ⓑ sharks   Ⓒ shrimp   Ⓓ deep-sea life
2. **What was used to see under water?**   Ⓐ flashlight   Ⓑ nothing   Ⓒ searchlight   Ⓓ telescope
3. **Living particles look like**   Ⓐ asparagus   Ⓑ footballs   Ⓒ snow-flakes   Ⓓ eggs
4. **At what depth in feet does darkness begin?**   Ⓐ 1300   Ⓑ 2300   Ⓒ 2500   Ⓓ 3000
5. **Shrimp flock to the**   Ⓐ light   Ⓑ torch   Ⓒ bathyscaphe   Ⓓ echoes
6. **The creatures at 2000 to 2500 feet down resemble**   Ⓐ eggs   Ⓑ asparagus spears   Ⓒ footballs   Ⓓ hatchetfish
7. **The shark's eyes were**   Ⓐ globs   Ⓑ glowing   Ⓒ gloomy   Ⓓ globes
8. **The sea's depth was about how many miles?**   Ⓐ 1   Ⓑ 3   Ⓒ 5   Ⓓ 7

No. right	1	2	3	4	5	6	7	8
G score	4.4	5.2	6.0	6.9	7.7	8.8	9.9	10.9

America, Plymouth Colony
April 1, 1621

Dear Richard,

The *Mayflower* carries a message back to you. We are now in America somewhere along the Atlantic, far enough north to have had a long, cold winter. Our voyage was hard and many times we threatened to turn back, but we kept on for several months before we reached shore. While we were sailing, some of the group from London threatened to go off by themselves in the New World, the land of no king and no laws. John Carver urged the settlers to cooperate in helping one another. As a result, all the men on the ship assembled in the cabin of the vessel before we landed and drew up a written agreement called the Mayflower Compact. Who do you suppose was elected governor? John Carver. In preparation for next winter we are making a storehouse, building homes with hewn logs, and planting enough Indian corn to feed the whole colony. This is the place for a courageous man like you and for a master mechanic. Come when the next vessel sets sail.

Your friend,
Samuel Fuller

1. **Who drew up the agreement?**   Ⓐ the men and women   Ⓑ some of the group from London   Ⓒ John Carver   Ⓓ the men on the *Mayflower*
2. **How did John Carver become governor?**   Ⓐ by law   Ⓑ the king appointed him   Ⓒ he got the most votes   Ⓓ he was the best master mechanic
3. **The voyage took**   Ⓐ all winter   Ⓑ several days   Ⓒ a few months   Ⓓ years
4. **Some threatened to leave**   Ⓐ London   Ⓑ the others   Ⓒ the *Mayflower*   Ⓓ the New World
5. **What did John Carver do?**   Ⓐ he threatened to turn back   Ⓑ he convinced everyone to stick together   Ⓒ he urged the settlers to write their friends to come   Ⓓ he went off by himself
6. **At the time this letter was written, the settlers were**   Ⓐ sailing somewhere on the Atlantic   Ⓑ planting food and building   Ⓒ writing the Mayflower Compact   Ⓓ assembling in the cabin
7. **The writer wants Richard to come because**   Ⓐ there is no king and no laws   Ⓑ the colony could use him   Ⓒ there was a place for him on the vessel   Ⓓ they had enough Indian corn
8. **What was the colony called?**   Ⓐ Mayflower   Ⓑ London   Ⓒ Plymouth   Ⓓ Fuller

No. right	1	2	3	4	5	6	7	8
G score	4.6	5.4	6.2	7.0	7.8	8.8	9.8	10.7

The discovery was entirely accidental. The two boys were searching for cattle that had strayed from the herd. The part of the plain over which they rode was separated from the inaccessible, and apparently useless, mesa by a turbulent stream. Jack had once seen a horse swim the river and disappear up the narrow box canyon of the mesa. Although the place had always been avoided by herders with cattle, the boys decided to cross and reconnoiter in search of the strays. They made their objective a high point that seemed to be the edge of the mesa. After an hour's climb they reached their lookout and beheld, in the cliffs above them, a city—a sleeping city of stone! There, nestled in a great cavern, beautifully proportioned and symmetrically made, was a village of little tinted, flat-roofed houses. "Mirage!" was their first thought. Then they realized that they were looking at the ruins of an ancient, extinct civilization. Preserved, in calm repose, were the homes of some of the forebears of our American Indians.

47

1. **The boys were looking for** Ⓐ a herd of horses Ⓑ a narrow box Ⓒ lost cattle Ⓓ a discovery
2. **What separated the mesa from the plain?** Ⓐ a trail Ⓑ a river Ⓒ a road Ⓓ a track
3. **Cattle herders always** Ⓐ kept away from the mesa Ⓑ crossed the stream Ⓒ climbed to a lookout Ⓓ disappeared in the canyon
4. **Who disappeared in the canyon?** Ⓐ four bears Ⓑ the strays Ⓒ Jack Ⓓ a horse
5. **What did the boys discover?** Ⓐ a pasture Ⓑ a plain Ⓒ a mountain Ⓓ cliff dwellings
6. **The writer says the city was "sleeping" because** Ⓐ everyone in it was asleep Ⓑ American Indians were living there Ⓒ they were tired out after their long climb Ⓓ it was completely deserted
7. **Which does not describe the city?** Ⓐ very old Ⓑ lightly colored Ⓒ finely made Ⓓ a mirage
8. **This discovery was not made before because the mesa was** Ⓐ uncultivated Ⓑ ancient Ⓒ isolated Ⓓ uninhabited

No. right	1	2	3	4	5	6	7	8
G score	4.3	5.2	6.0	7.0	7.9	9.0	10.1	11.2

48

Last winter, before a crowd of sightseers, a sixteen-year-old Indian boy subdued alligators. To mystify the tourists, he called this procedure "hypnotism." First he crawled into a pen containing a hundred or more alligators and asked a man in the crowd to select the animal to be hypnotized. On the day I was watching, the one selected was about five feet long. The boy quietly separated it from the others by steadily following it and finally, on reaching an open space, he placed himself directly in front of the alligator and tried to seize its jaws. In doing this, he was very careful, for the animal has a powerful tail stroke which can quite easily knock a man down and inflict painful injury. After the boy had firmly clamped the jaws together with his hands, he turned the animal on its back. As the alligator had become somewhat tired by this time, it was a fairly simple feat.

Since an alligator is helpless on its back, the boy now began softly stroking the creature on its throat and chest. In a few minutes, it was perfectly quiet and apparently had ceased breathing. The boy declared that the only way to waken the alligator was to give a peculiar call. This he gave in a very soft voice. The animal's throat muscles began to pulsate noticeably. Then the boy turned the alligator over on its feet, whereupon it moved quietly away.

The spectators, not knowing that the nerve centers of alligators are in the breast, were mystified and astonished at the performance.

1. **Alligators have very strong**   Ⓐ eyes   Ⓑ backs   Ⓒ tails   Ⓓ feet
2. **The boy managed to**   Ⓐ subdue the alligator   Ⓑ astonish the alligator   Ⓒ mystify the alligator   Ⓓ select the alligator
3. **The feat was performed**   Ⓐ for Indians   Ⓑ for tourists   Ⓒ for Americans   Ⓓ by the alligator
4. **The alligator to be hypnotized was selected by**   Ⓐ the boy   Ⓑ me   Ⓒ an Indian   Ⓓ a tourist
5. **An alligator on its back, as compared with the same alligator on its feet, is more**   Ⓐ powerful   Ⓑ helpless   Ⓒ wriggling   Ⓓ vicious
6. **One could tell the alligator was becoming more active by the**   Ⓐ throat   Ⓑ opening mouth   Ⓒ pulsating chest muscles   Ⓓ peculiar call
7. **The nerve centers of the alligator are in the**   Ⓐ head   Ⓑ tail   Ⓒ back   Ⓓ chest
8. **The Indian boy was**   Ⓐ very surprised   Ⓑ brave   Ⓒ hypnotized   Ⓓ a spectator

No. right	1	2	3	4	5	6	7	8
G score	4.4	5.3	6.0	7.0	7.8	8.9	10.0	11.1

Will Scarlet told Robin Hood of a fat, merry monk called Friar Tuck. "He has never been beaten with bow or quarterstaff," said Will. Robin Hood was eager to have such a skilled man in his company, so, taking his bow, he set out with fifty of his men to visit the friar.

When Robin arrived on the bank of a stream, he heard Friar Tuck humming merrily near by. "Now for some fun," Robin said as he hid his men.

"Come and carry me across the water, good friar, or it will be the worse for you," said Robin Hood.

"Since I am a friar, it is my duty to help the weak," said Friar Tuck, bending down for Robin Hood to clasp his broad shoulders. With Robin on his back, the friar waded across the stream, the water at times higher than his waist.

Robin Hood laughed all the way across the stream. Then Friar Tuck set his "passenger" down on the bank, jerked out his sword, and Robin Hood was at his mercy.

1. **Who had never been beaten?**   Ⓐ Will Scarlet   Ⓑ Friar Tuck   Ⓒ Robin Hood   Ⓓ the fifty men
2. **What did Robin Hood carry?**   Ⓐ a bow   Ⓑ a gun   Ⓒ a knife   Ⓓ a flag
3. **What did Robin Hood hear someone doing?**   Ⓐ singing   Ⓑ calling   Ⓒ crying   Ⓓ humming
4. **What did Robin Hood plan when he saw the monk?**   Ⓐ revenge   Ⓑ fun   Ⓒ a confession   Ⓓ robbery
5. **Where were Robin's men?**   Ⓐ hiding   Ⓑ in the stream   Ⓒ at Friar Tuck's mercy   Ⓓ home
6. **How did Robin get Friar Tuck to carry him?**   Ⓐ by beating him   Ⓑ with his sword   Ⓒ by threatening him   Ⓓ by asking nicely
7. **How did the friar cross the stream?**   Ⓐ on a bridge   Ⓑ by jumping   Ⓒ by swimming   Ⓓ by wading
8. **Robin Hood's main purpose when he set out was to**   Ⓐ have some fun   Ⓑ cross the stream without getting wet   Ⓒ get Friar Tuck to join his band   Ⓓ avoid being captured

No. right	1	2	3	4	5	6	7	8
G score	4.2	5.0	5.8	6.8	7.6	8.7	9.9	10.9

"Now," said Friar Tuck, "it's *your* turn. Carry me back or you will feel the point of this good sword." This Robin Hood was forced to do. It was hard work for him, because the friar was very heavy and the stream was full of holes. Angry and sweating, Robin Hood reached the bank, grabbed his sword, and cried, "Now *I* have *you*! Carry me back again!"

The monk was getting angry, but he was forced to bend his back. On reaching the middle of the stream, he gave a sudden jerk. Robin tried to grab the monk, but in vain. He fell into the stream with a huge splash. The monk waded back toward his dinner.

Robin Hood was furious. He rushed on the friar with his sword. They fought for six hours, breathing in gasps.

Robin, forced to admire the pluck of the friar, fell on his knees, saying, "I beg a boon of you, holy friar."

"What boon?" asked the friar.

"That I may blow three blasts on my horn."

"Certainly," said the friar, "and I hope you blow so hard that your eyes pop out."

1. **The bed of the stream was full of**   Ⓐ fish   Ⓑ mud   Ⓒ holes   Ⓓ stones
2. **Carrying the friar was**   Ⓐ hard   Ⓑ exciting   Ⓒ easy   Ⓓ pleasant
3. **At what part of the stream did the monk give a jerk?**   Ⓐ the middle   Ⓑ the shallowest   Ⓒ the muddiest   Ⓓ the clearest
4. **How did Robin Hood feel?**   Ⓐ silly   Ⓑ enraged   Ⓒ huge   Ⓓ certain
5. **Who waded back toward his dinner?**   Ⓐ Robin Hood   Ⓑ the one who was dumped into the stream   Ⓒ one of Robin Hood's men   Ⓓ Friar Tuck
6. **How many hours did Robin Hood and Friar Tuck fight?**   Ⓐ two   Ⓑ four   Ⓒ six   Ⓓ eight
7. **Robin Hood admired the monk for his**   Ⓐ weapons   Ⓑ long gown   Ⓒ courage   Ⓓ weight
8. **Robin asked Friar Tuck for**   Ⓐ a horn   Ⓑ a bone   Ⓒ a favor   Ⓓ a sword

No. right	1	2	3	4	5	6	7	8
G score	3.3	4.0	4.8	5.8	6.8	7.8	9.0	10.2

Robin Hood blew three blasts on his horn and his fifty men hurried to him.

"Give me a boon," said Friar Tuck, "just as I gave you."

"That is only fair," said Robin Hood.

The Friar blew his whistle three times, and fifty great dogs came racing. Two dogs attacked Robin. One tore the green cape from his back. He had all he could do to keep the other from his throat.

The outlaws, seeing their leader in danger, began shooting arrows at the dogs. Soon Little John, a deadly shot, had accounted for a dozen. To prevent more of his friends from being killed, Friar Tuck cried, "Stop, good fellow, stop!" Then the friar called off the dogs, and the fight ceased.

Robin Hood told the friar that he had come to ask him to join his band of merry men. The friar laughed heartily and was well pleased with Robin Hood and his archers. He agreed to join the outlaws and soon became the beloved friend of them all.

1. **How many of Robin Hood's men appeared?** Ⓐ twenty Ⓑ thirty Ⓒ forty Ⓓ fifty
2. **How many of the friar's followers came to him?** Ⓐ twenty Ⓑ thirty Ⓒ forty Ⓓ fifty
3. **What was the color of Robin's cape?** Ⓐ yellow Ⓑ red Ⓒ green Ⓓ brown
4. **Robin tried hardest to guard his** Ⓐ throat Ⓑ arms Ⓒ legs Ⓓ shoulders
5. **How was Robin Hood's joke on the friar turning out?** Ⓐ badly Ⓑ amusingly Ⓒ the way he wished it Ⓓ merrily
6. **How many dogs did Little John kill?** Ⓐ none Ⓑ twelve Ⓒ twenty Ⓓ fifty
7. **Robin Hood described his men to Friar Tuck as** Ⓐ happy Ⓑ brave Ⓒ beloved Ⓓ good
8. **Which of these is the best title for this part of the story?** Ⓐ Where Joking Pays Ⓑ The End of a Rivalry Ⓒ Fifty Faithful Dogs Ⓓ Little John's Deadly Aim

No. right	1	2	3	4	5	6	7	8
G score	2.7	3.6	4.6	5.8	7.0	8.4	10.0	11.5

52

If someone should tell you that there is a fire inside you, and that this fire is keeping you warm, you might think it was meant to be a joke. But that is pretty nearly what is taking place.

Most of you know that a fire will burn only when plenty of air is supplied. The oxygen of the air combines with the carbon of the coal or wood and gives out heat. In like manner, the oxygen taken into the body through the lungs unites with the carbon of the muscles and other parts of the body, producing heat that warms the body. You do not see any fire in the body because the oxygen unites with the carbon so gradually that only sufficient heat is produced to keep the temperature of the body at about 98.6 degrees.

If the temperature of a healthy body rises above the normal 98.6 degrees, it is automatically cooled off. If you have ever dipped a thermometer in gasoline or chloroform and watched it while the liquid was evaporating or drying off, you will understand how the body is cooled. While the liquid is evaporating, the temperature falls very rapidly, often from five to ten degrees in as many minutes. Nature has a similar method for cooling the body. When the little particles of water called perspiration are evaporated from the skin, the body is cooled to 98.6 degrees.

1. **To have a good fire you must have**   Ⓐ muscles   Ⓑ a thermometer   Ⓒ air   Ⓓ coal
2. **The part of the muscles with which oxygen combines is**   Ⓐ water   Ⓑ carbon   Ⓒ blood   Ⓓ fat
3. **The selection states that the heat in the body is produced by**   Ⓐ uniting of oxygen with carbon   Ⓑ heat in the radiators   Ⓒ heat of the sun   Ⓓ plenty of clothing
4. **A thermometer is used to measure**   Ⓐ degrees of heat   Ⓑ light   Ⓒ rainfall   Ⓓ humidity
5. **While liquid is evaporating on a thermometer, the temperature will**   Ⓐ go up   Ⓑ go down   Ⓒ stay at 98.6 degrees   Ⓓ fall below normal
6. **Perspiration on the body is caused by**   Ⓐ drinking too much cold water   Ⓑ eating too much food   Ⓒ the production of excess heat in the body   Ⓓ falling temperature
7. **What happens to your body when your temperature goes above normal?**   Ⓐ there is a fire in your body   Ⓑ you perspire   Ⓒ it needs oxygen   Ⓓ the temperature falls 5 to 10 degrees in as many minutes
8. **Evaporation from the skin causes**   Ⓐ coolness   Ⓑ heat   Ⓒ fog   Ⓓ humidity

No. right	1	2	3	4	5	6	7	8
G score	3.8	4.7	5.7	6.8	7.8	9.2	10.3	11.7

The bat uses its ears much as we do our eyes, to avoid collisions. Watch a bat early some summer evening. How fast he flies! Yet he seldom hits an object. Stretch fine wire between trees. He will not strike the wires as he flies. He does not see the wire either in light or in darkness. He hears it. We look about us as we move rapidly, so that we will avoid obstacles. The bat listens for them. How? As he flies he makes shrill noises rapidly. His ears can hear them, but yours cannot. The bat can tell by the echo where an object is and how close to him it is. Think of all the sights and sounds around you that you never see or hear!

Observing the bat's method and making use of radar, scientists have invented a small box for the blind to carry. As the blind person approaches an object, his earphones, attached to the box, buzz. The length of the buzz tells him how near to the object he is. Thus, the blind person "sees" with his ears, in somewhat the way a bat does.

1. **The bat seldom hits an object when he flies because he** Ⓐ feels it Ⓑ sees it Ⓒ hears it Ⓓ smells it
2. **What kind of noises does the bat make?** Ⓐ loud Ⓑ high and sharp Ⓒ trilling Ⓓ soft humming
3. **The bat can tell where an object is by** Ⓐ the buzzing Ⓑ earphones Ⓒ echoes Ⓓ wires
4. **This story tells how science has** Ⓐ improved nature Ⓑ destroyed nature Ⓒ applied nature's principles for human use Ⓓ learned little from nature
5. **This invention that aids the blind is the result of** Ⓐ scientific research Ⓑ the study of the eye Ⓒ rapid shrill noises Ⓓ fine wires
6. **The invention helps the blind** Ⓐ avoid collisions Ⓑ keep away from bats Ⓒ see with their eyes Ⓓ carry boxes
7. **The blind can tell how to avoid an obstacle by** Ⓐ a fine wire between trees Ⓑ the length of the buzz Ⓒ the loudness of the buzz Ⓓ the sights and sounds around
8. **This invention makes use of** Ⓐ bats' sounds Ⓑ radar Ⓒ fast flying objects Ⓓ light and darkness

No. right	1	2	3	4	5	6	7	8
G score	4.9	5.7	6.6	7.4	8.4	9.5	10.4	11.5

54

Do you have a savings account in a bank? Do you know what the bank does with your money?

Suppose you put $10 in your savings account. The bank does not keep that money. The bank will loan the $10 to somebody else. When a person borrows this money, he or she promises to give back more money than the bank loaned. Suppose that somebody borrowed your $10 from your bank. That person might promise to give the bank $11 at the end of one year. This extra one dollar is called interest.

The bank uses part of the interest it gets to pay the people who work in the bank. Another part is used to pay for telephones and electricity and other such expenses. Still another part is given to the people who own the bank. The largest part of that one dollar, almost one half, is given to you. You see, you were loaning the $10 to the bank. So, the bank pays interest to you. Of course, you can also get your $10 back.

1. **When you put money into your savings account, the bank** Ⓐ keeps it in a safe Ⓑ loans it to somebody else Ⓒ uses it to pay for electricity Ⓓ gives it to the bank's owners
2. **When a person borrows your money from a bank, he or she** Ⓐ promises to give you more money back Ⓑ promises to give the bank more money back Ⓒ promises to give the bank $1 Ⓓ promises nothing
3. **The extra amount paid to use somebody else's money is called** Ⓐ a promise Ⓑ borrowed money Ⓒ a savings account Ⓓ interest
4. **The people who work in the bank are paid from** Ⓐ the money you put into the bank Ⓑ borrowed money Ⓒ the interest the bank gets Ⓓ the interest you pay
5. **If you put $10 in a savings account, you will get back** Ⓐ more than you put in Ⓑ expenses Ⓒ $10 Ⓓ less than you put in
6. **Out of every dollar the bank gets for letting somebody use your money, you get** Ⓐ $10 Ⓑ nothing Ⓒ about one half Ⓓ $11
7. **The bank gives you more money than you put into your savings account** Ⓐ to pay for the telephones and electricity Ⓑ because you are loaning the money to it Ⓒ only if you work at the bank Ⓓ only if you own the bank
8. **If a person borrowed $10 from a bank and the bank wanted to get back $11 at the end of one year, how much do you think the bank would want to get for a two-year loan?** Ⓐ $12 Ⓑ $21 Ⓒ $22 Ⓓ $11

No. right	1	2	3	4	5	6	7	8
G score	3.5	4.3	5.3	6.5	7.6	9.0	10.4	11.9

You eat lamb and wear woolen clothes because there are sheep and a shepherd and sheep dogs. If the shepherd did not have a sheep dog, he would need to hire twenty or perhaps fifty helpers to do the work the dog does with a large flock.

When I was in England, the shepherds of Scotland had brought their most intelligent and best-trained sheep dogs down to London to compete for the national prize. One of the many contests was to see how quickly each dog could separate a group of sheep and drive them through a gate.

These dogs also keep the sheep off the roads and out of big timber. If a single sheep is lost, they know it and search until the lost one is found. If a sheep is crippled or a lamb is too weak to walk, the dog will stand by it and bark until the shepherd comes.

1. **Sheep dogs are** Ⓐ dangerous Ⓑ affectionate Ⓒ lazy Ⓓ dependable

2. **We have warm clothes to wear because of** Ⓐ a dog Ⓑ a shepherd Ⓒ sheep Ⓓ shepherds, sheep, and sheep dogs

3. **The shepherd's dog can do the work of how many men?** Ⓐ a few Ⓑ several Ⓒ twelve Ⓓ fifty

4. **Why were the shepherds in London?** Ⓐ to see who had the most sheep Ⓑ for a contest Ⓒ to be trained Ⓓ to drive through a gate

5. **The aim of the contest was to choose the best sheep dog in** Ⓐ the nation Ⓑ London Ⓒ England Ⓓ the United States

6. **The contests aimed to see which dog could** Ⓐ jump the highest Ⓑ run the farthest Ⓒ manage the best Ⓓ see the best

7. **The sheep dog will bark if** Ⓐ a sheep is lame Ⓑ the shepherd is weak Ⓒ he is on the road Ⓓ he wants to go out of the timber

8. **If one sheep is lost, the sheep dog** Ⓐ knows and searches Ⓑ stands and barks Ⓒ runs in circles Ⓓ hunts for the shepherd

No. right	1	2	3	4	5	6	7	8
G score	2.8	3.7	4.7	5.9	7.2	8.7	10.3	11.9

56

In 1916, the worst college football defeat in history took place in Atlanta, Georgia. Georgia Tech beat Cumberland 222–0, and it took them just 45 minutes to do it.

Wilt "The Stilt" Chamberlain set a National Basketball Association record by missing 22 free throws in a 1967 game.

It took 7 hours and 23 minutes (23 innings) for the San Francisco Giants to finally win over the New York Mets, 8–6, making the 1964 game the longest in baseball history.

In 1900, the first organized automobile race in the United States was held, and the winner, A. L. Riker, covered 50 miles in 2 hours and 3 minutes in an electric car.

In 1894, Montreal defeated Ottawa 3–1 in the first Stanley Cup hockey match. Canada's Governor-General, Lord Stanley, donated the cup, which cost $48.66. It is priceless now.

1. **Choose the best title:** Ⓐ Unusual Sports Records Ⓑ Baseball, Football, Basketball, Hockey, and Racing Bests Ⓒ The Old Days of Sports Ⓓ How Athletics Have Developed
2. **Which of these events took the shortest time?** Ⓐ the hockey match Ⓑ the automobile race Ⓒ the basketball game Ⓓ the football game
3. **How much is the Stanley Cup worth today?** Ⓐ $48.66 Ⓑ $1,894 Ⓒ nothing Ⓓ more than anyone can pay
4. **Wilt Chamberlain set a record by** Ⓐ beating the Giants 222–0 Ⓑ missing twenty-two baskets in one game Ⓒ playing the longest game in basketball history Ⓓ winning the first organized car race
5. **Mr. Riker drove** Ⓐ less than 25 miles per hour Ⓑ 50 miles faster than the electric car Ⓒ 1900 miles Ⓓ from Montreal to Ottawa
6. **In the longest baseball game,** Ⓐ Canada beat the U.S. Ⓑ the Giants beat the Mets Ⓒ it took 2 hours and 3 minutes to go 23 innings Ⓓ the score was 3–1
7. **Who gave hockey the Stanley Cup?** Ⓐ Wilt Chamberlin Ⓑ A. L. Riker Ⓒ the Governor-General of Canada Ⓓ Lord Cumberland
8. **Which of these events took place most recently?** Ⓐ the automobile race Ⓑ the football game Ⓒ the baseball game Ⓓ the basketball game

No. right	1	2	3	4	5	6	7	8
G score	5.6	6.3	7.1	7.9	8.9	9.9	10.8	11.8

There are many ways in which we can be peacemakers. One way is to tolerate the opinions and desires of others. Many quarrels result from arguments in which people become angry with the opinions others express. Many religious wars have arisen because one party would not tolerate the beliefs of others. We all have a right to our opinions. However foolish an opinion may seem, we should allow it to be expressed, and should not take offense because others do not think as we do.

Quarrels arise because our desires conflict with those of others. At home two people sometimes desire the same thing, and neither will give way to the other. We should be willing to give in to many of the desires of others. Unselfishness promotes peace. If all of us are willing to let others have their fair share of things, and their own place in games at home and at school, we can live in peace.

1. **One way to be a peacemaker is to** Ⓐ tolerate quarrels Ⓑ become angry Ⓒ agree with the opinions of others Ⓓ be tolerant of the opinions of others
2. **Quarrels arise because two people** Ⓐ hold different opinions Ⓑ express different opinions Ⓒ will not listen courteously to each other's opinions Ⓓ hold foolish opinions
3. **The writer says we should always let others** Ⓐ have their own way Ⓑ have their fair share Ⓒ have whatever they want Ⓓ play any game they wish
4. **Which statement is true?** Ⓐ Peacemakers cause quarrels. Ⓑ Quarrels cause intolerance. Ⓒ Unselfishness and tolerance promote peace. Ⓓ Differences of opinion cause unselfishness.
5. **Choose the best title:** Ⓐ Conflict in School Ⓑ Selfishness Ⓒ Keeping the Peace Ⓓ Religious Wars
6. **It is wrong to** Ⓐ desire the thing another desires Ⓑ be unwilling to listen to another Ⓒ be tolerant Ⓓ differ from another in opinion
7. **If someone has a foolish opinion, they should** Ⓐ not be listened to Ⓑ be allowed to say it Ⓒ fight for it Ⓓ tolerate religion
8. **Which statement is true? Everyone** Ⓐ has the right to a fair share and place in society Ⓑ has to play games Ⓒ takes offense Ⓓ should always give in to others

No. right	1	2	3	4	5	6	7	8
G score	3.5	4.4	5.5	6.6	7.8	9.3	10.6	12.3

58

Most of us have read the legend of Hiawatha in Longfellow's poem, but few know that the real Hiawatha was one of the statesmen who founded the Iroquois League, or Five Nations.

In the days of Hiawatha, the Iroquois tribes had engaged in fraternal warfare until reduced to want and misery. Hiawatha and another chief called a council that established the League of the Iroquois and abolished war among them forever. The league was democratic. Its chieftains were elected. No war could be waged without the consent of all the nations that were members. Any outside nation could have peace with the Iroquois by becoming a member. Later, the league became the Six Nations.

The Iroquois, now transformed from weak tribes into a powerful nation, conquered all Indian peoples who dared to attack them. Their great domain separated the French colonies at Quebec from those on the Mississippi. By keeping apart these colonies, they enabled the British to conquer Canada.

The league founded by Hiawatha remains the heritage of his people.

---

1. **Who was Hiawatha?**   Ⓐ a legend   Ⓑ a long fellow   Ⓒ an important leader of his people   Ⓓ a big league player
2. **Before the League of the Iroquois, the tribes**   Ⓐ fought with each other   Ⓑ wrote poems   Ⓒ reduced want and misery   Ⓓ got engaged to be married
3. **They formed the league in order to**   Ⓐ call a council   Ⓑ stop all wars between themselves   Ⓒ go from Quebec to the Mississippi   Ⓓ fight the French
4. **Who chose the chieftains?**   Ⓐ Hiawatha   Ⓑ Canada   Ⓒ everyone who voted   Ⓓ the side that won the war
5. **An outside tribe could have peace by**   Ⓐ reducing the Iroquois   Ⓑ joining the league   Ⓒ conquest   Ⓓ waging war
6. **After the tribes became the Six Nations, they were**   Ⓐ weak   Ⓑ very strong   Ⓒ destroyed   Ⓓ separated
7. **All their lands stretched from**   Ⓐ Britain to France   Ⓑ Quebec to the Mississippi   Ⓒ the French colonies to Canada   Ⓓ Britain to Canada
8. **Hiawatha is**   Ⓐ remembered and valued by his people today   Ⓑ only a legend to his people   Ⓒ forgotten   Ⓓ found by the Five Nations

No. right	1	2	3	4	5	6	7	8
G score	6.7	7.3	8.0	8.9	9.8	10.4	11.3	12.2

The skyscraper, which is one of the greatest modern American creations, came into being as a result of necessity. The demand for room in an already congested district made it necessary, and modern engineering methods made it possible.

The steel-cage system of construction makes the superstructure possible. The cage is made of steel beams fastened together with bolts. It may be compared to a bridge set on end. The steel skeleton forms the whole support for the upper floors, and the walls are merely covering for protection.

The construction of the substructure is just as marvelous. It must be so built that it will not only support the superstructure and its contents, but also bear the pressure exerted upon it by the force of the wind against the walls. In building the foundations, steel caissons—large boxlike structures—are sunk down to bedrock. When they reach bedrock, the rock is leveled and the caissons are filled with concrete; thus solid piers are made from bedrock to the surface of the ground.

1. **The skyscraper was constructed because of**   Ⓐ the shortage of space in cities   Ⓑ substructures   Ⓒ steel   Ⓓ caissons
2. **The steel beams are fastened together with**   Ⓐ bolts   Ⓑ boxes   Ⓒ concrete   Ⓓ steel cables
3. **The steel cage may be compared to**   Ⓐ any bridge   Ⓑ a concrete bridge   Ⓒ a railroad bridge   Ⓓ a bridge on end
4. **The walls of the skyscrapers are used primarily**   Ⓐ as support for upper floors   Ⓑ for protection   Ⓒ as caissons   Ⓓ to give architectural beauty
5. **The support of the upper floors of the superstructure is directly dependent on**   Ⓐ the walls   Ⓑ the steel skeleton   Ⓒ concrete piers   Ⓓ steel caissons
6. **The cage is made of**   Ⓐ bars   Ⓑ solid piers   Ⓒ steel beams   Ⓓ walls
7. **What must the substructure do?**   Ⓐ be a boxlike structure   Ⓑ support the superstructure   Ⓒ have a skeleton   Ⓓ provide a covering
8. **What does the wind do?**   Ⓐ turn the engineering machinery   Ⓑ press against the walls   Ⓒ put pressure on the bedrock   Ⓓ exert force on the substructure

No. right	1	2	3	4	5	6	7	8
G score	5.9	6.6	7.4	8.1	9.2	10.0	10.8	11.8

60

Many times in the past, Arctic ice has crushed down over parts of Europe, Asia, and North America. Why has this happened? And why are layers of coal found in Antarctica?

Great mountain ranges, such as the Rockies and the Andes, have been raised. What caused these mountains to rise and new seas to invade portions of the land?

Once, in ages past, millions of mastodons and other types of animals met sudden death. During summer months many centuries ago, vast numbers of mastodons were frozen solid. Summer plants have been found in their teeth and stomachs. The meat of mastodons dug from the frozen earth is still edible. What great catastrophe deep-froze these animals?

Geologists have developed a theory that may explain all these mysteries. Place a weight on one side of a sphere, spin it at high speed and the sphere will fly into many pieces. The great Greenland icecap and the larger icecap on Antarctica are not centered on the Poles. They cooperate to put great strain on the surface of the earth. About every 20,000 years this strain causes the thirty-mile-deep surface of the earth to slip on the molten rocks below. From time to time, points on the earth have moved as much as 2,000 miles from their previous positions. Great earthquakes, like one in Assam that raised Mount Everest more than a hundred feet, indicate that the earth's surface may be about to move again.

1. **A mastodon is** ⒶⒶ a mountain   Ⓑ an extinct animal
   Ⓒ a geologist   Ⓓ a tooth
2. **Geologists are**   Ⓐ mystery writers   Ⓑ scientists who study the
   earth   Ⓒ developers of the deep-freeze   Ⓓ people who explain dead
   animals
3. **If you place a weight on a sphere and spin it at high speed what will
   happen?**   Ⓐ the weight will break into pieces   Ⓑ a great
   catastrophe   Ⓒ an earthquake   Ⓓ the sphere will disintegrate
4. **Two icecaps mentioned are**   Ⓐ Andes and Rockies   Ⓑ Everest and
   Assam   Ⓒ Greenland and Antarctica   Ⓓ Europe and Asia
5. **How deep is the earth's surface?**   Ⓐ 20,000 miles   Ⓑ 2,000 miles
   Ⓒ 30 miles   Ⓓ 100 feet
6. **What happens when there is a great strain on the surface of the earth?**
   Ⓐ it centers the Poles   Ⓑ there is cooperation   Ⓒ the surface slips
   and moves   Ⓓ Mount Everest is raised
7. **The surface of the earth moves**   Ⓐ only in the mountains   Ⓑ every few
   years   Ⓒ about every two hundred centuries   Ⓓ 2,000 miles from
   Assam
8. **The earthquake at Assam indicates that the earth's surface may move**
   Ⓐ soon   Ⓑ in another 20,000 years   Ⓒ in a hundred years   Ⓓ in the
   summer

No. right	1	2	3	4	5	6	7	8
G score	4.6	5.5	6.6	7.6	8.9	10.2	11.5	12.9+